Triggered ReActions Conquered

Written By: Lisa Hopkins

Copyright © 2022

All Rights Reserved

Publisher: The Mason Publishing Company

This Book contains privacy of the author you cannot copy or duplicate this book all rights reserved. No part of this publication may be reproduced, stored in a retrieval system, or transmitted in any form or by any means -electronic, mechanical, photocopy, recording, or any other- except for brief quotations in printed reviews, without the prior permission of the publisher. For information address Themasonpublishingcompany@gmail.com

printed in the United States of America

ISBN: 978-0-578-27631-1

Table Of Contents

Title Page

Copyright..1

Table Of Contents................................2

Acknowledgements..........................5

Dedication..6

Introduction...8

Chapter 1. Grandpa Again....................10

Chapter 2. Church.................................29

Chapter 3. Help Me Jesus....................41

Chapter 4. Military................................49

Chapter 5. Crack Addiction & The

Marriage...84

Chapter 6. Nervous Breakdown…………...…**139**

Chapter 7. Lynda…………………………….**156**

Chapter 8. Apple Valley……………….……**186**

Chapter 9. Fugitive……………………….....**203**

Chapter 10. Frankie……………………..........**212**

Chapter 11. Crack At Church……………....**237**

Chapter 12. Family……………………….......**249**

Chapter 13. Hope For A Future……………**268**

Chapter 14. Charles Walker………………....**270**

Chapter 15. Scriptures Of Apology………..**274**

Chapter 16. Substance Abuse………………..…**282**

Chapter 17. Thank You Lord.........................**293**

Chapter 18. Poem: Jesus Conquers All…...**301**

Declaration..306

Concordance Scripture Reference Page.......308

Acknowledgements

To my mother Helen Ford, my father Willie James Hopkins, his wife Carol Hopkins, My grandmother- Willie Juanita Cryer /Ford Apostle Sandra L Hanna, Sam and Patricia Harris, Charles Walker, My Pastor, and church family.

Dedication

This book is dedicated to my wonderful mother Helen Ford For all the love that she has shared with me throughout my lifetime. I would like to pay homage to my beautiful mother for all her support down through the years, for always loving me when I didn't know how to love myself. Mommy, I LOVE YOU

To my Children

Isaiha, Asia, Ivan, Imyunic

This book is also dedicated to my loving children for loving me and allowing me to be the best me I can be. My journey to this point has been rough, each of you had the opportunity to see me come out of my mess, I'm grateful for each one of you. May you follow Jesus Christ as Lord and Savior in these last and evil days, now and forever till we meet on the other side.

I LOVE YOU

Introduction

My Innocence, gone at 10 years old. Rape, molestation, alcoholism, lies, abomination, confusion and insanity. Just to name a few circumstances that I had encountered. It all started when I was 10 years old. How does a person overcome this type of turmoil, what would I have to do to endure. Should I run and hide, bury my face in the sand with my hands on top of my head. Many have had challenges in life that they had to overcome. I am sharing very intricate portions of my life. This is an effort to prove that there is hope for a future of success. Easy does it, and timing is everything. With God all things are possible. There is peace for your times of despair.

Chapter 1

Grandpa Again

"Here we go again, he's in my room touching me again." "Why won't he just stop?" In my innocence at 10 years old I realize that maybe it's not so bad, in fact I liked it, that one thing he did with his mouth. For one week he was in there, in my room and in my bed every single night. I realized it was a feeling that me as a little girl, and my innocence never wanted to not feel. In fact, when he didn't come into my room it absolutely made me angry. I'd be rolling my eyes at him throughout the day, and he would know he made me feel some type of way. I can recall all the lies he used to tell me to keep me content." If you tell anybody they will not believe you." "If you don't tell I'll buy you a car when you graduate high school." "It's OK if we have sex, we're not really related, your mom was switched at birth. Naturally, I believed every bit of it, because this was my grandpa.

Grandma and grandpa did not sleep together anymore, he'd have to come out of his bedroom, pass my grandma's room, go out the back door and around down through the driveway, and with his keys he'd open the front door where I slept. It is proven that this man was totally insane. There were pertinent reasons why he did the things he did and said the things he said, he was an alcoholic and nothing he said or did made any sense. Grandpa was a very smart man, he had a number of skills and was able to teach his children to always work and make a living for themselves, in fact he told my aunt Evelyn to learn how to type, and who would have known that she would become a stenographer, when she got older, she worked in the courthouse in downtown Los Angeles. My grandma was the sweetest ever, she was a seamstress and made clothes for many people. No matter what grandma did, she was everything to me. Grandma could make chicken that was out of this world, we would have chicken dinner every Sunday. I could talk to my grandmother about anything, but this one thing about what her husband was doing to me could not get out. How could I tell my grandma that I asked grandpa for a banana, and he told me to take two so that I could eat one. I did not understand that at the time, but he was implying that I could eat one of the bananas and use the other one on myself for sexual gratification. Grandpa and grandma had five children between the two of them. Evelyn Ford who has grown up to be a stenographer. Helen Ford who was my biological mother. Helen works for the school board in Los Angeles unified school district for 25 years and retired. I was born in 1967 to Willie James Hopkins of Jackson Mississippi and Helen Ford of Chicago Illinois. Melbourne Ford who joined the Military, Annabel Ford who watched grandpa give encouragements to her older sister to learn to become a secretary told her to get out of the room because what they were doing did not concern her. Well, that did not bother Annabelle she figured out how to learn that typing skill and worked in various arenas becoming head secretary. I am so grateful that she did not let grandpa make her feel like it did not concern her because she made sure that it did. Henry Ford was the last of grandpa and grandma's children he did 7 years in The United States Navy, and he is an impressive photographer. Grandpa's name was Collins Ford and grandma's name was Willie Juanita Cryer-Ford.

You might ask where my mother was the whole time all the child molestation was going on with me when I was a child. Well, to be quite frank about my mom was suffering with her own issues because of her dad which was my grandpa, the same sick individual that had me dazed and confused. When my mom was 25 years old on one occasion, I was told that grandpa took his own daughter, my mom into his room to have sex with her. Mom siblings heard her hollering and screaming grandpa to stop. Sometimes she didn't come out for more than an hour. Of course, during these times, you would think that grandma would have intervened, I'm sure she knew what was going on during all those times grandpa was doing things, I believe she was afraid to say something or even to protect her own. Of course, I was not born yet while my mom was having her issues with rape and molestation, but you can believe that I sure wanted to know why she allowed me to stay in the house with my grandparents at any time. I had a long-time resentment towards my mother for leaving me to become a victim of my grandpa. Later I came to find out that Mom had a nervous breakdown, and there was nowhere else for me to go. I had not started going to visit my dad yet, and he did not know what was going on. Day after day for 5 more years grandpa would drink more, and he kept coming in my room and doing what he did with his mouth. As my body developed from a caterpillar to a little butterfly grandpa continued to have his way with me and my grandma never said a word and neither did I. When I got to junior high school my mom was better, she had her own place for a while, and I went to live with her. It really wasn't my plan to go live with her, it was grandpa's. It really was grandpas....Why? I'm glad you asked, it was a beautiful day and I had just gotten out of school got home, rang the doorbell, and grandpa open the door to let me in, as I began to walk in the house, he grabbed my breast so hard to my reflexes cause me to slap him over the sewing machine. He was so angry, and nobody knew it except for me. He did not tell anybody and neither did I. The next day when I went to school and got back home grandma told me that I was going to have to move out because grandpa said they had already raised their own children, and that they were getting older, and they needed to spend time alone together in their old age. It was a crock of bull, because grandpa was angry and embarrassed and that was the first time, I had ever struck him because of his misbehavior toward me. I went to live with my mother.

Child molestation is a crisis in every community. Those who commit this at all very sick people. Child molesters are not only old men who prey on kids. There are women that do it, young men do it. Family members do it to their young, and predators of all nationalities are committing acts of child molest station every day. Child moleststation is known as sexual abuse often used with manipulation, lies and false promises. Kids are people too, and they cannot consent to any form of sex. It is wrong and sometimes the kid does not really know what is really going on. Child molest station can have a long-lasting effect on those who have been victimized. The victim does not even have to be touched to be targeted.

Touched and Untouched

Fondling

Oral sex

Intercourse

- Exposing oneself

- Obscene conversation

- masturbation

There are plenty more activities that a predator could do, Will do and have done then these that I mentioned. If you suspect that a child is being molested, because of different behaviors, physical signs, using words or phrases that are too adult for their age, or unexplained silence. Please talk to the child. Pick a safe place where the child is comfortable. Be aware of the tone that you use when speaking. Ask questions that match the child's vocabulary. Listen closely, avoid judgment and blame, be patient, and make sure the child knows he/she did nothing wrong. One of the main things is to be very patient with the child. If the truth comes out immediately report it to the police, hospital, or whoever can help with the needs of the child. Child protective services my aid and removing the sexually abused child from the home if the assault occurs where the child resides. call or text child helpline national abuse hotline at one

800 422–4453, you will reach a trained volunteer or crisis counselor. The counselor can make a report or suggestions for you. National sexual assault hotline can also be utilized at 1 800 656 HOPE or chat online@online.RAINN.org. Please try to educate your children about child predators and child Molestation. We must protect the children from those who set out to harm them by the act of child molestation and sexual abuse. Let's see what the Bible says about child molestation.

1.) Matthew 18:6- But whoso shall offend one of these little ones which believe in me, it was better for him that a millstone be hanged about his neck, and that he was drowned in the depth of the sea.

2.) Ecclesiastes 4:1 -So I returned and considered all the oppression that done under the sun and behold the tears of such as were oppressed, and they had no confidence, and on the side of their oppressors there was power, but they had no comforter.

Galatians 5:19-21 now the works of the flesh are evident sexual immorality, impurity, sensuality, idolatry, sorcery, enmity, strife, jealousy, fits of anger, divisions, envy, drunkenness, orgies, and things like this I warn you, as I want to be for that those who do such things will not inherit the kingdom of God. In other words, God is not pleased with this type of behavior, it is an abomination, and it stinks in the nostrils of God.

"OMG, I just heard the back door slam, he is on his way. Around back and down the driveway to the front door of this house, key turning and into my room. Grandpa again!!!

Chapter 2

Church

Living with mom was not so bad, I went to Bret Harte junior high school, and I was a good student. Every day it bothered me to know that nobody but me and my grandpa knew why I had to move out and go live at my mother's house. I had started going to visit my dad from time to time and getting to know his side of the family. It was cool, I came to realize that my father side of the family was much bigger than my mother side of the family. My dad 's family had a family reunion he took me to several reunions out of state and to visit the local relatives. My very most favorite auntie was my aunt Dorothy. My aunt Dorothy was really into church and the things of God. You could call her a woman after Gods own heart. Aunt Dorothy came and picked me up one day for church. The name of the church I attended was Greater Bethany Community Churuh under the leadership ship of (Bishop RW McMurray) Aunt

Dorothy was an alter call worker, therefore since she was in the business of leading people to Christ of course she asked me if I wanted to receive Jesus Christ as Lord and Savior. Of course, I did want to receive Jesus as Lord and Savior and that is what I did and a couple of weeks later I receive the gift of the Holy Ghost speaking and other tongues as the Spirit of God gave utterance. I came to really enjoy going to church, I had joined the Mass Choir as well as the children's choir called the chosen generation. Soon after I had to start riding the church bus so Aunt Dorothy would not have to go out of her way to pick me up. I really enjoyed being a member of a church and having a church family. I knew that Jesus was real, and I wanted him in my life. riding the church bus was not bad at all. It was a big blue and white bus like a school bus. I met some of the people that rode the church bus as well. Everything was going good. Church was helping me to not think about my childhood and everything I went through at grandpa's house. As many may know, anytime a Christian is trying to do the things of God the enemy, which is the devil will come in like a flood to wreak havoc. One Sunday on the way home from church my friend Kay asked me if I had a boyfriend. I told her no, and asked her if she had a boyfriend, she said" No" and declared that she did not want one. She said she did not like boys and that she wanted a girlfriend. I asked her why, and what could she do with a girl. she said, "I would hold her hand, kiss her, take her places, and lick her down there." Oh my God, I thought about grandpa licking me down there and how much I liked it. This woman asked me if I wanted to be her girlfriend and I said yes without a second thought. K lived around the corner from grandma and grandpa. I figured out a way to move back in with my grandparents because by this time I was ready to start 10th grade and John C Fremont high school was just down the street from grandma's house. My grandparents did not have a problem with it. Grandpa never thought about touching me again, but he still did and said things that were inappropriate. It did not bother me, I had too much schoolwork to worry about and of course now I had a girlfriend. Grandpa was always sticking his nose and some business that had nothing to do with him. When I was little when he first started touching me, I can recall a time where he took me and three of my boy cousins out to the back house and taught us how to have sex. We were kids we did not care about that. when I had my first sexual encounter with K unbelievably grandpa was looking through the window on the bedroom door. He even opened the door and looked in and started Orchestrating what we were already in control of. we did not need his added two cents. I should have gotten in trouble, but no he was enjoying looking at what he saw. when it was all said and done, he never said a word about it ever. One Sunday after church K and I was sitting on the porch just talking about random stuff, Here comes my uncle Henry with his camera." Hey you guys want to take some pictures? "Of course, we do, we need some pictures together. K had already graduated from high school and me not giving a thought to it, I took all the pictures that I thought I want it to take. We took pictures holding hands, holding each other, me in front of her and even a kissing pic. The pictures came out nice after they were developed. In fact, one day I took those pictures with me over to my aunt Rose's house. The pictures were in my back pocket, and I asked my cousin and my aunt if they wanted to see the picture of my boyfriend. They said yes and we're looking at K and yes, she looked like a boy, and they were convinced that I had a boyfriend. Later that day my cousin Lena came over and my Auntie said," did you show Lena your boyfriend? "I said no not yet, but when I did show her the picture, she knew exactly who it was. I was busted. My cousin Lena said," that's not no boy, that's K she lives across the street from my boyfriend 's mother 's house. At that moment I knew my family knew that I was a lesbian. Lena told her mother, and her mother told my dad. In fact, Aunt Rose told my dad that K was already 18 years old and had graduated from high school and she was considered an adult and was committing statutory rape. My dad told them that I was going through a phase and to leave me alone. This lifestyle went on for many years after that. The police were never contacted, and I was glad about it.

Church Bus

Big Blue

Chapter 3

Help Me Jesus

Rape, molestation, alcoholism, abomination, lies, confusion, and insanity. these are just a few of the circumstances that I had already experienced at such an early age. John 1:1-In the beginning was the Word, and the Word was with God, and the Word was God. I wish I had known this at an early age. Everybody must bring everything that is not of God about themselves to God When they except Jesus Christ as Lord and Savior. Many times, and in most situations, people do not receive Jesus Christ as Lord and Savior and automatically change overnight, some things must be worked out of a person over time, through prayer, or maybe cast out by prayer and fasting. Many people never overcome everything that they have ever gone through. We lean and depend on God for spiritual guidance through His Word, Faith to believe His Word is true. While walking by faith and not by sight. In the last two

Chapters we saw how the enemy took over and had me indulging in situations that I had no business. I was an innocent kid and someone who I was supposed to trust took advantage of me. There is so much rape, child molestation, manipulation and whatever goes along with it. It's a sad shame that an adult would take advantage of a child and use them for their own sexual gratification. Many things that I had gone through were unnecessary. I was a young kid in the beginning, and I did not know how to use the word of God as a weapon. Today I lean and depend on God for everything, and trust Him to lead, guide and direct me in the right path for my life. God is faithful, who will not suffer you to be tempted above that which you are able but with every temptation God will always present you with a way of escape that you may be able to bear it. 1Corinthians 10:13, The Lord is not slack concerning his promises, as some men count sickness, but long suffering to us-ward, not willing that any should perish, but that all should come to repentance.

2nd peter 3:9. I thank God for salvation, and I do not regret anything that I have gone through. In fact, I am grateful that the Lord allowed me to go through it and blessed me to still be here. My troubles and trials have made me the woman that I am today. I give thanks in all things all circumstances for this is the will of God in Christ Jesus for you and me, all of us. 1st Thessalonians 5:18. The Bible tells us to train up a child in the way that it should go and when it is old, he will not depart from it. Proverbs 22:6 I thank God that I was brought up in the church, although I had so many things going on. The Word is true, because I am a living witness of the child that did not depart from the word of God. When the enemy came in like a flood, the Spirit of the Lord lifted a standard against him on my behalf. Isaiah 59:19. Although I had gone through so many tricks of the devil, God was there with me, He was my protector from the evilness in my grandfather. Galatians 5:10 says to have confidence in the Lord, that He will be none otherwise minded, but he that troubles you and he shall bear his judgment whosoever he be.

This means that those who take advantage of Gods precious little ones will be punished. The Lord is my shepherd I shall not want, he makes me to lie down in green pastures, he restores my soul, He leads me in the path of righteousness, for his name's sake, yea though I walk through the valley of the shadow of death I will fear no evil, for thou art with me. He prepares a table before me in the presence of my enemies. He anoints my head with oil. My cup runneth over. Surely goodness and mercy shall follow me all the days of my life, and I will dwell in the house

of the Lord forever.

Chapter 4

Military

I graduated from John C Fremont high school in 1986. I was a happy camper, now striving to figure out this thing called life. Mom told me when I asked about money for college that there was none. In other words, I was on my own trying to figure it out. One day I woke up and said," I got it, I'm going to the military." I sought out to figure out what I had to do to be accepted into the United States Navy. After I did, I was on my way. January 7, 1987 was the first day of Boot Camp. Boot Camp was eight weeks long, and I absolutely hated it. Boot Camp was very strenuous at times, and most of the time nerve-racking. I pressed on smartly. I ended up doing an extra week because I could not fold my dungarees properly. Oh yes, I could go to the gas chamber where the gas was escaping, learned how to protect myself just in case there was Gas escaping in a confined space, but no, I could not fold those dungarees properly. I got recycled and had to do a full week over. Upon completion of that week, I was on my way to my Boot Camp graduation. The motto was, "If you can make it here, you'll make it anywhere." I believed it whole heartedly and I believed in everything that I had learned and that it would take me as far as I would let it. We were taught to stay ready, so we did not have to get ready. Of course, I never made it to the war, fortunately it wasn't war time. There were many soldiers that were stationed all over America and overseas. Not Lisa, I was on a dry dock ship, stationed on full duty as a United States Navy fireman apprentice. I had all the rights and privileges of every other soldier. I thought that everybody was my friend, and that I was well liked. Well, soon came to find out that it was not true. Once I got the hang of working with others, learning the 3M systems, and having the ability to complete assignments on my own, I felt good about being in the United States Navy. I was stationed at Little Creek amphibious base which was in Virginia. I was 19 years old, and I did not know anything about Virginia. I was blessed because my stepmothers father lived in Virginia Beach, Virginia. He was married and had three boys. I became a part of the family, and I am so gracious to them. To this day shall I always be a part of the Byers family. The name of the ship I was on was called Mobile Diving Salvage Unit Two. I worked there, I slept there, and I ate there, and it was the place that I called home. I lived on the ship for a year and six months, I enjoyed it, I got used to sleeping on the middle rack, it was like a bunkbed that had three beds. I got tired of it after a while, I was able to move into my own apartment off base if I wanted to, but Mrs., Byers told me if I moved off base to come to live with them in their house. For me that was out of the question. I chose otherwise, I got my own apartment. I moved to a complex called Botanical Gardens. I had my own car, my own place and my own space. I was good at my job and was feeling very comfortable about my life. I had been on the job for about one year and six months and I knew that when I did start my family that I could also steer them in the direction of going to the Military. I was a Hull

Technician. My job was nothing more than being a plumber on the ships system. "If you have a plumbing issue and you need it fixed right away, call on fireman apprentice Hopkins. "We at mobile Diving Salvage Unit Two we're also working with a diving salvage team. They would recover things found in the ocean waters near the ship and would report the findings. They would also have special operations at times according to what their supervisor requested of them, while taking necessary actions, we'd have to help the divers get ready to do their diving and help them get out of diving gear as well. It was our duty to clean all diving gear and put it in its proper place making sure everything was ready for the next day of use. On the ship we used a system called 3M maintenance management, it merely taught us how things were supposed to be cleaned on the ship. In the military I learned to use a P250 De watering system which was used to dewater a flooded space. We'd have practice tests to insure that we knew how to put it together, properly break it down, and properly restore it to its compartment. We also learn exercises and techniques to ensure that we were ready in the case of a real emergency. One day we did have a real emergency. It was flooded in the men's sleeping quarters." "Hopkins! get the hoses and man the dewatering system." "Flooding male sleeping quarters, forward ship." "Sir yes sir" I commenced. When the job was done it was time to break everything down and store the P2-50 dewatering systems motor mount for the hoses away. Everybody had gone and I was left there to put the heavy system away by myself. I saw some sailors passing by, and I asked them if they would help me carry the system to its proper compartment. One of the male sailors said," if you can't manage your job young lady, then you need to get out of my navy." I got so upset that I picked up this very heavy equipment, threw it over my shoulder and started to carry it. I felt something knot up in my stomach and I was on my way to the hospital. Three days later I had an umbilical hernia repair. I had gone on light duty, and I could only work on the ship mostly making plumbing repairs and cleaning.

Recovery was great and when I went back on full duty, I was convinced that I could be even better at what I was trained to do, it was not the young man's Navy only, it was my Navy as well. One day after a hard day's work I went home, prepare dinner, watch some television, prepare for work for the next day and went to bed. Everything was good till I got to my car. My windshield was shattered, my front passenger tire was flat, and my left driver side back tire was also flat. I felt so scared, wondering who had done this and why. What did I do to deserve this. Mind you, I am only 19 years old and what I will soon find out is going to blow my mind, literally. I did not know what to do, but I knew that I had to get to work. I was sure that my car wouldn't make it, and I'd be late. There is no such thing about not showing up to military duty. I had to get there the best way I knew how, I took a bus, and I was an hour and 20 minutes late. On the ship when a sailor is late or a no-show. That seller would have to go speak to their immediate supervisor, and the supervisor was mandated to send a service member to the executive officer of the ship. You were in big trouble; some incidents could even need you to captain's mass. Captains mass is like going to civilian court. Heavy charges could send someone to the brig. The brig was military jail. Fortunately, the executive officer understood that I had a major issue. I told him what had happened, and I was excused and went on about my workday. I was still puzzled all day long about what had happened to my car while I was sleeping. Today is a new day, it is Friday tomorrow would be the day that I get my car damages fixed. The next day was Saturday, as I got ready to take the car to the automotive place I walked out of my apartment, turned to lock my door, and noticed these symbols directly written on my door. I thought, what now? I had an appointment that I did not want to be late for. I decided to take a piece of paper and draw those symbols on it. I folded the piece of paper up and put it in my back pocket. When I got to the automotive place I checked the car into them, sat down and really tried to figure out what was written. I pondered in my mind about what these symbols and signs were. I asked the young man at the counter if he had ever seen anything like it? His response was no. My car was fixed, and I was on my way back home. It was still light outside so I took cleanser and soapy water and tried to remove the symbols. I had left the original paper that I used to copy the symbols on in the car so that I could ask around on the ship on Monday. Monday morning, I discussed it with my supervisor, unfortunately he had never seen anything like it before. I asked a couple of fellow workers, and low and behold someone knew what it was. Petty officer Gray was his name, and he asked me why I had this paper. I told him that I woke up a couple of mornings ago and these markings were all over my door. He said," where do you live Hopi?" Oh, Hopi was my military nickname. I told him that I moved to botanical gardens, he said Hopi you should have never moved there."" That's where the Ku Klux Klan have their meetings, they do not want you there, and you will never know who they are because they were plain clothing. The young man looked serious, and I did not know what to do next. it was at that moment that I knew that I should have listened to the Byers, My newfound family. Mr. Byers told me, DO NOT move off the ship, if you must please come and live with us." I knew I had made a terrible mistake. I loved my little apartment, but I knew I would have to move out to make sure that I'm safe.

Since I was young and really didn't know what to do, I knew that I had to be at work on time daily, and that my work ethics had to still be continuous and up to par. That only lasted for about two weeks, suddenly I had become critically concerned about the happenings in my life. I had begun to get nervous, paranoid and I did not know who to trust, in fact I didn't trust anyone. I could not trust my supervisor, nor those who I consider my closest friends. Everything was going downhill quickly. To the point that when people merely said good morning it would irritate me so bad, I would tell them "Don't speak to me you're probably the one that's doing it!" Or someone would ask me a question and I wouldn't even say a thing, I'd give them a nasty look and keep on walking. I found myself wanting to be by myself, and work alone. I made every effort to be by myself so much to the point that I would only talk to myself. I didn't trust anyone so therefore I did not interact with anyone during work, or otherwise. Once during the day, a man who worked in another department put his hand on my shoulder and asked me how it was going. I yelled at him from the top of my lungs and told him please do not put your hands on me, and I began to cry, and I ran off to my supervisor and told him that I was a nervous wreck and that I needed to take the rest of the day off. He allowed me to go home, and it was a good thing it was Friday the day it was over anyway. I had the weekend to regroup and try to relax after preparing for the coming week. Monday when I got back to work, I was told by my supervisor that I needed to report to the nurse's station. The nurse was contacted about what had happened on Friday. The nurse also knew that I had my issues, and it was told to her that my attitude and actions were progressively getting worse, and no one understood what or why these things were going on. Quiet as it is kept, not even me. I had no understanding of how I wound up all the way in Virginia. I felt like I had been hoodwinked and swindled mainly because it was all another trick of the devil. I was a victim of prejudice, and it was the first time I had ever gone through anything like that. The nurse wanted to know what happened from start to the present. It was right at the beginning of December and then annual reports were due, people were preparing for a test to get promotions to go up in rank. The ceremony was going to be on December 20 just before Christmas and everybody who was to be elevated would be, but not me, I got sent to Portsmouth Naval Rehabilitation center. Lisa Hopkins was admitted to mental health. I was really a person with real mental health issues, I could not believe it during my stay at the hospital, I began to wonder what I needed to do to get out of the military and go home. I was convinced that I was defeated, and I was ready to give up. I knew that live in the US Navy was not something that I wanted to continue. I was on the last day of my treatment for mental health. I had spent 13 days already and was scheduled to go back to work in two days. When I got back to work, I was heavily medicated. I only had one day to be at home before I had to be back at work. A week after being at work I realized that because of the medication that I had to take every day that was prescribed for my mental health issues my work ethic was no longer good. I couldn't think, I was still paranoid, having crying spells, and just wanted to go home. I had to figure out a way to get out of the United States Navy. Day by day for the next two weeks everybody was a suspect and whoever was responsible for the things that happened to the car and the symbols on my door were on that ship. I still did not trust anyone. When I got so overwhelmed, I went to the executive officer's quarters to ask straight out if I could go home. He wanted to know why, and I told him that ever since the visit to the mental health hospital I did not feel like I could really be a productive anymore. I told him that I was really having a problem trying to figure out how to do the things that I had already learned to do. I knew how to do plumbing on a ships system, But I could not quite figure it out anymore. I told him that I feared that I would hurt myself or someone else in the process of doing my daily routines as I had always done before with no problems. I told him that I couldn't concentrate on the tasks that I was asked to do, I would literally forget what to do next. To me I was a danger to myself and others mentally and physically where it pertains to work ethics, and the quality of my work was decreasing daily. The executive officer told me that he would look over my medical records and get back with me in two weeks. It was four days before Valentine's Day when the executive officer called me into his office, I was sure that he was going to let me go home. The executive officer told me that when he had looked in my medical records it was not enough for me to be discharged, therefore I was to continue full duty until my military assignment was over. Every single day I cried and was very paranoid. A lady who worked with me asked me why I was always crying, I told her because "I want to go home" she said," don't you know if you went to the captain's office and told the captain that you were homosexual, he would have you on the first thing smoking out of here. "Lord have mercy, I could not believe it". I immediately went to his office, knocked on his door, salute him and said," Captain I came here today to discuss the military 's policy on homosexuality" He said," Why? "Are you homosexual" I said "Yes" he said," well, fireman apprentice

Hopkins, we do not allow homosexuality in our United States Navy, I'm going to have to discharge you. This will not be a dishonorable discharge; it will be a general discharge under honorable circumstances." My flight left Virginia on February 14th, 1989. I left my apartment just like it was, and my car was shipped to Los Angeles, and active duty in the United States Navy was behind me forever. You would think being in the military is the best thing that could happen to anyone. Unfortunately for me it was not a great position to be in. Being a victim of prejudice is so sad. There has been prejudice for many years. I was born in 1967, I honestly thought I had missed it. I did come to learn that there was a lot of prejudice still going on in Virginia. It was not war time, And I should have had a peaceful experience. I knew that everything that I was going through that God was with me. I needed Gods Peace, I had it according to the Word of God. Peace, I give to you, I do not give to you as the world gives. Do not let your heart be troubled, do not be afraid. The word of God tells us that He gives us our peace and we do not have to be afraid. I truly was afraid when I was in the military, it was another tactic of the enemy! I felt like I was having troubled times, that I wasn't going to make it, like I was in a war. It was a battle of my mind; I had no peace. I could not sleep, I could not eat, I could not think all because I had no peace. Today I do have peace, the Word of God tells me that there is neither Jew nor Greek, there is neither bond or free, there is neither male nor female, we are all one in Christ Jesus. Galations 3:28. So if that be the case why did the ignorant sailor boy have the right to tell me that it his Navy. The word of God is true, I just wish I knew the word back then like I do now. The word of God in Acts 10:32 says Peter open up his mouth and say it, I truly understand that God shows no partiality. Sailor boy should not have been partial to me just because I was a woman. When I was in the Navy, I did not know anything about the Word, but I came to find out the protection, peace, and love is found in the word of God. For God is love. A new covenant have I given onto you, that you love one another as I have love you. Found in John 13:34, now if God is love and we are supposed to love one another, then the young man was not showing me any love. Although I have gone through so much in the military, I knew that God was with me through it all. I needed a relationship with God, that way I could recognize when the enemy was doing something against God's will. Behold I stand at the door and knock. If anyone hears my voice and opens his heart, I will come into him and sup and He with me. Revelation 3:20 I am so glad that Jesus now lives in me. When troubled times come, I can call on the name of Jesus, He will answer me and come to my rescue. Although I know we must suffer to reign with God. He will never put more on us than we can bear. I know that the race is not given to the swift nor to the strong, but it is to the one who endures until the end. I sure wanted to make the military my career goal. I wanted to tell my children how the military could be a great career for them. unfortunately, I did not get to share that story. I am grateful to the military today; I suffer from post-traumatic stress disorder and the military

is paying for it 100%.

January 7th, 1987_ February 14th, 1989

Mobile diving savage unit 2

Hull Technician

Little Creek Amphibious Base, Norfolk, Virginia

Chapter 5

Crack Addiction & The Marriage

Landed in Los Angeles, California on Valentine's Day, February 14th, 1989. I called Carol, who was my dad's wife. I told her I had just landed at the airport, and I was no longer in the Navy. The next question was could I come stay at their house until I could get me a place. Of course, the answer was yes, but they did not know what the future would hold. My dad and my stepmother lived really close to the airport, so I only had to wait for them to pick me up for a short while. No one knew why or how I got out of the Navy, and I never told it. I figured since I had plumbing experience already that maybe I could go into the plumbing business. I would purchase a van and fill it with all the compartments for the tools and parts that I needed to do plumbing jobs with. I would hire two or three young men that may already have experience, or they just graduated from plumbing school. I would even hire somebody that was down on their luck and had the skill as a professional and was out of work. It was a dream to on my own company and retire at the appropriate time. I'd send the workers out, they'd do the job, The customer would pay me, and I would pay them. Unfortunately, it did not happen that way. Everything was going good far as my living arrangements, but one day here comes my auntie silver fox. It was good to see her, and she was the type of person that was here and there and everywhere, she was very street-smart, knew all the tricks of the trade, and a natural born hustler. In times past, I had never known Auntie silver fox to ever have a real 9-to-5 job, but she was never broke. One day auntie Silver Fox asked me for a ride to a friend's house not too far away. When we got there, she got out of the car, knocked on the door and went in. I sat waiting for her for almost 30 minutes. I got tired of waiting, so I knocked on the door and asked where my auntie silver fox was. The lady of the house kitty king of whom I had never met took me to where Auntie Silver fox was, and asked me if I wanted to get something? "Something like what?" I asked, she said," some smoke" I was looking at auntie silver fox and she was looking at me. She looked like she was very loaded and high as a kite. When I saw her, she was looking and acting weird, I should have said, "Hell no!!," I was so curious, took the bait, and asked how much did it cost? Kitty king said you can spend what you want to. So, I handed her a $50 bill and before I knew it, I had taken my first hit of crack cocaine. Lord have mercy, what have I done. It was the best feeling you could ever feel, at least this is what I thought.

Coming out of the Navy I had plenty of money. The really bad thing about it all was I was only three weeks out of the Navy, and I was strong and high every day after that for a long time. My family always could tell when I was sober and when I was high. After that first all- nighter, I stayed high for the next five years and I had a child every year during those five years. in 1990 my whole thought process had become corrupt, I had to learn new ways of getting money, I was having sex with random men, and everything that came out of my mouth was a lie. I had the crack demon living inside of me. The addiction of crack Is a foul spirit, A strong hold something you cannot shake easily. Like having a monkey glued to your back. I had no self-control, I was not wise in my decision making, cleanliness and hygiene did not matter, and getting the next hit was the only thing that was important. I didn't have the willingness to do anything right. I lived on 107th St. and Figueroa, so naturally I walked up and down Figueroa. Figueroa Street was known to be the street that prostitutes went up and down to get money for sex. The people believed that I had become a prostitute as well, but to keep it 100% I had tried to turn my first trick on Figueroa Street, that night I wound up getting in an unmarked police car with an undercover police officer. I was on my way to jail for the very first time in my life. I was so scared. It was easy breezy I got out in two days and was on my way to the crack house. Mind you it was the best experience because it let me know that I didn't want to be a prostitute; because prostitution could have taken me to a place that I didn't want to go, that could have been jail, prison or death. I left prostitution up to the pros. The ones who knew what they were doing. One day while I was walking down Figueroa, I met a man. He worked at a place called Central Rentals. Just before I passed the company, a tall, handsome, and Caucasian gentleman called me. I have never given him the time of day, but I had seen him in the past. His name was Mr. Walker. We talked for a while, and he invited me to lunch, scheduled for the next day. I did not turn down the offer, nor did I know where this lunch date would lead to.

The next day Mr. Walker took me to a nice restaurant in Marina Del Rey. One week later after we had been talking on the phone in the evenings when he was off work, he offered me money for sex. So, I was seeing him every other day for $100, then I was able to use that money to get high. I absolutely enjoyed meeting Mr. Walker on Monday, Wednesday, and Friday. this arrangement lasted for about a little over a year. Mr. Walker always treated me with love and respect. Mr. Walker was one of a kind and he was so sweet and thoughtful. The only thing that was really an issue, that to me really was not an issue, was the fact that I was loaded every day and Mr. Charles never knew. Yes, I was thankful for that. One Friday evening when Mr. Walker got ready to drop me off, he said," hey sweetheart, I think I'm falling in love with you. "Mr. Walker pulled a ring out of his pocket and asked me to marry him. There must have really been something there for him in my heart as well, because I started to cry, and said," yes! yes" "I will marry you." We planned a date. Called my aunt Dorothy to be our witness and we went down to the courthouse in Los Angeles California, and we got married. The question is, did we live happily ever after? Mind you I was pregnant when we got married, but I did not know if it was Mr. Walker's baby or not. Mr. Walker and I never became an exclusive item while we were dating. He was my trick. l was having sexual relations with a guy on 104th St. The baby was born May 5, 1990. We named him Isaiha Walker. My aunt Lenore gave Isaiha his middle name (Ahmed). Unfortunately, when Isaiha was born, he was drug addicted, when the social worker from the hospital came in and told me, they did not immediately take my son from me she told me that if I could get clean within 60 days that I could keep my son. I had to go and drug test whenever they called me in. I never knew when I would test, and I really didn't take them that serious. One day the worker called me and Charles in for an evaluation to talk about how well I was doing. At least that's what I thought. I had given a dirty test two days after the 30 days was up. The worker looked at Isaiha and said," Look how cute and healthy he is may I hold him?" I handed her the baby, and just like that the baby was getting taken away from me. Charles could not get the baby, because in a court of law when they did the paternity test, he was deemed not to be the father. I cried like a baby, and so did Charles. Fortunately, Isaiha went to my dad's house, and I was able to see him whenever I wanted too. The judge told me That I had to go to a drug program and complete six months of it to get my child. I was so addicted, out of control and spun out until I could not meet the requirements. On December 24th, 1991, I had my second child, and again it was not my husband's baby. From the hospital they took Asia and Carol my stepmom and my father James had custody of my second child. Still, it did not matter to me I was addicted to something that had complete rule over my whole life by now. I felt bad every single day that I have betrayed my children in this way, in fact I felt so bad that I could not even face them, I did not know how to act around my children. These babies were innocent, and like the old saying says, they did not ask to be here. The cycle continues day in and day out the same old mess. Crack addiction had gotten the best of me, and the cold thing about it is I was not tired of ripping and running the streets, and looking crazy in the face, and treating my husband like he didn't matter either. Charles was a good man. It was like I couldn't do anything to make him angry. Not that I was trying to, but he always showed me love no matter what. I can recall the third time I got pregnant, and no it wasn't his child. I came in the house and Charles was sitting on the bed. I sat down next to him, and I began to cry, he puts his arm around my shoulder and says," what's the matter sweetheart, did you go out there and get yourself pregnant again? "that's exactly what happened". Charles showed no anger, he said don't worry sweetheart we will take care of the kids. I thought how we are going to take care of the kids when they keep taking them. This time Carol and James my stepmother and father did not get my son when he was born. His name was Ivan Edwards, and his dad was Lancy boy…

The dude on 104th St. OMG!!! Remember The commercial about the baby that couldn't take the hit. That baby had so many tubes connected to it, oxygen, and some more stuff. That baby was so tiny you could hold it in the palm of your hand. Guess what? My baby was the same way. Ivan weighed 1 pound and 8 ounces, and yes, I could literally hold him in the palm of one of my hands. He was so tiny and extremely sick on top of the fact that he was drug addicted at birth. Ivan did not get to go where my other two children were, he was sent directly to foster care.

He became the 98th child that these foster parents had. A year later I had another baby that was not Charles's and that child also went to the same foster home as their 99th baby. That was my fourth child that was born drug addicted and that I did not have at home with me. I was a terrible parent and a terrible person all the way around. Four children that I did not have custody of. Four children that didn't even know me. Four children that I am sure had issues that I caused. I had to do something I had to get these children back into my custody. I had to wake up and try at least. One would wonder where was I having all this sex at year after year with these different men. How is it that I had time to be with other men and slept in the bed with Charles every night. Charles and I lived in Inglewood about 12 minutes away from my dad's house. Two blocks from the house where the motel that I used to hang out. I would go to the motel every morning when Charles would go to work. I would stay there until he got off work. I wasn't going to the motel to have sex with people, I was going to the motel because I didn't want to use drugs in the house. Ironically, I called myself not wanting to disrespect the house or my husband. Well, that was an oxymoron because I was disrespecting him by having all these children that were not his, but that was the way I thought besides, I did not want my husband to know that I was using crack. How I held it from him for so long I will never know. I'm sure he must've had an idea. One day he comes in the house and calls me over and tells me that his friend told him that I was hanging out at the hotel. It wasn't enough for him to just say it or to ask me was it true, he asked me," so what are you doing at the hotel are you letting people buy pussy off yah?" Oh, my goodness you will never know or understand how angry I got. I cursed at him. He wasn't wrong to be thinking that because after all when we first got together that's how it was with, he and I. No that wasn't the case and never had I ever gotten pregnant by anybody at that hotel. I told Charles the reason why I was at the hotel was because I was trying to respect him and our home because I had a drug addiction problem. It was the first time he had heard that I was drug addicted because it was the first time, I had ever said it. I told him "Since you think I'm selling myself then guess what???"" I will just smoke my dope right here in the house. Whether you are here or whether you're gone it does not make me no difference I don't want to keep running down the street anyway and why should I have to when I have a home. "Mind you I had done nothing to try to get the kids and my drug addiction piped up another notch and went to a whole nother level. I started hanging out back over there off

Figueroa Street near where my first two children were at with my stepmom and my dad. Right back to Miss Kitty King 's house. Luckily, I still had my car so I could make my moves and get home before Charles. Let us not forget that Charles worked on Figueroa as well. Charles has stopped giving me money when he found out that I was using. That was the worst thing you could have ever done because I have never for the last four years had to hustle to get money for drugs. auntee-silver fox still hung out at kitty king's house. Day in and day out the hustle was on, and it was real. on a beautiful summer day in Los Angeles California the actual dope man asked me if he could use my car. It was the first day of the month and everybody was waiting on their checks well at least silver fox, and I were waiting on our checks. We had to wait for the mail carrier to run and I thought well if I give the dope man the car, we'd have something to do while waiting for the mailman to run. Auntie Silver Fox told me, "Don't give up the car we're going to need the car when the checks get her." it was already too late I had the smoke, gave auntie silver fox some as well. The lady of the house. While I was getting loaded, I got word that my car had been in an accident. I immediately reported the car stolen. The guy/dope man went to jail and when the court date came, I saw him outside of the courthouse and he asked me to drop the charges. He said if I did, he would give me more crack. Sounded like a great deal to me so I went for it. I never had time to see about getting the car out of the impound to get it fixed, or to use my insurance to get my car fixed. I do not know if there was such a thing because in all actuality, I gave the car to the dope man. I could have reported the car stolen gotten a police report to go with it. Didn't sound like a good idea to me because I was loaded what would I look like going to the police high as a kite. Sounds like grounds for my arrest, I wouldn't have had my story together and it would have been a whole lot of malarkeys. I left it alone and continued with my day. Mind you I don't have a car now, so I guess I'm going to have to take my husband's car. After all auntie Silver Fox always assured me that we'd have money if we had a car. I arranged with Charles that I would drop him off in the morning to his job and pick him up after work. By this time Charles had gotten a new job at a college. He was the night custodian. I'd drop him off, after work at pick him up, and he would drop me off at the house. Whatever money I had I would use it to get loaded until Charles pulled up in the driveway. By this time, I wasn't even having sex with Charles anymore. Not because he did not want to but because his schedule was so full that when he came home pulled up in the driveway, I would have already taken my shower, so that I could just jump in the bed and make it seem like I was sleep. I can recall when me and Charles first started dating and he told me that he would get me anything I wanted. I knew that I could get another car, and that he would buy it for me. The only thing wrong with that situation is that I did not have time to go sit at the car lot and do all the necessities that I had to do to get this car, so I put it off for a long time. I felt like as long as we had a car everything was good in fact, one day I decided, hold up let me back that up, I was loaded one day, and I was supposed to pick Charles up and since it was on a Friday, I figured he could get home the best way he knew how. What a rip off, and that it really was. Charles called me and asked me where I was, I told him that I was stuck at someone's house, and I couldn't get out because the police were outside of the house getting ready to do a raid on the house. Charles made it home and he called me and told me that he was going to call off work at the college to make sure that I am all right. Charles asked me when I was coming home, and I told him I'll be there as soon as I can. Well, I never went home I got so consumed with getting loaded that I lost track of the time, Charles got angry and call the police. The next day I was driving the car and he had the police put an all-points bulletin out on the car I heard it over the radio and parked the car and got out. This was on a Saturday. The car was still parked where I parked it. to make sure that Charles wasn't so mad at me I told him where the car was and where I had left the keys. Charles asked me when I was coming home, and

I told him I did not know because I had got arrested and I was calling from the jail. Charles asked me if I needed money and I told him no, and that I would be OK and the only reason I'm in here is because I was driving under the influence. Well, Mr. Charles was the type of man who was going to see about Lisa no matter what. The next day he went to the jail, and he asked if he could see me. Lisa Walker, Low and behold when Lisa Walker came out to see Charles Walker it was a messed-up ordeal. "Well why was it so messed up Lisa?" I am glad you asked!

Well, I had lied about going to jail. I needed to buy some time so that I could sober up enough to go home and look Charles in his face after I had stolen the car. I had gotten myself in a world of trouble so that was a for sure way to weasel my way out of something by lying. I just told Charles that they let me out before he got there, and for his questions I had no answers, I had already told all the lies I was going to tell about being in jail. The following weekend Charles took me to lunch, it was a Saturday before Sunday church. Yes, I was getting high on

Saturday and was still going to church on Sunday. Saturday was the day Charles and I spent quality time. I was still a member at Greater Bethany Community Church of Los Angeles, And Charles was a member of another church. He was the minister that would take the money home because he was supposed to put it in the Bank the following the next day. Well, that Monday when Charles went to get the money from under the mattress to go to the bank the money was gone. The reason it was gone is because I asked my husband if he had some money and he told me "NO" Well it didn't matter if he did or didn't, but I knew there was no way that Charles could be broke. He was never broke, he just wanted to tell me no because he knew that I wanted it to get loaded. He lied to me. Of all the lies that I had ever told, I had the nerve to get mad because Charles told one lie that I did not even know if it was a lie or not. I was out to prove a point. The point was, "Now you don't have no money," because I got it. I was a happy camper it was $220 in that envelope that came from the church. I had no shame, and I didn't care where it came from because if it was in his possession to me, it was his. I even had the nerve to ask him what he was going to do, and how was he going to put the money in the bank if he did not have any. He let me know that he was going to go to the bank and pull it out of our account and put it in the churches account. I looked at him and said "Liar," went and took a shower and went to bed. Charles left the next day for work and did not leave me any money. I looked on the bed, on the floor, under the pillow, in the bathroom, there was no money for Lisa. Charles has the car, and I was stuck in the house. I thought" how is he going to switch up and not leave me with some money." "He got me messed up. I got up, got myself together and left the house. Yes, I did do something strange for a little change that day. I got loaded and hung out the rest of the evening. When Charles got home, I was not there. I did not come home until it was about time for him to go to work the next day. I crawled my little musty butt in the bed. I didn't give him a chance to express how he felt about me staying out all night, or otherwise before I said to him," Charles are you going to leave me some money today. Charles didn't say anything, he threw me a $20 bill and walked out the door. Well $20 was never enough. I opened the front door, threw it out, and told him I didn't need his money and that I would get my own money by any means necessary. I was not going to be responsible for the outcome. When I got myself together and got ready to leave the house the $20 was down the hallway nobody had touched it. That was great,

(My Beloved husband of 19 years)

I could catch the bus. I'll go hang out off Figueroa Street. This day I went to see my children Isaiha and Asia. I spent most of the morning with them. While I was there, I had a conversation with my dad, he told me that I needed to get myself together because my children were going to have to start school soon. At least my firstborn, Isaiha. I was sitting on the porch with the children and just enjoying their company thinking about calling Charles and telling him to pick me up on his way home. Here comes the enemy, it was the guy two houses down from my dad, his name was Mr. Brown, he was standing in his yard telling me to come here. I did not know what his deal was, he was a married man, and I knew it, and still went to see what he wanted. I never knew this man was a crack addict, but he told me that he had some crack, and he didn't want to get high by himself. The one day that I was trying not to get loaded, I got loaded. Me and the young man had sex and we commenced to smoking. Suddenly, this dude says," Oh my heart, I think I'm having a heart attack call the paramedics. "I thought to myself what the heck have I gotten myself into?" I told him to give me the crack if he thinks he's going to the hospital. This dude told me when the paramedics leave, come back. Well, I never did go back, I took my butt home and mind you I did wind up getting that crack to take home with me. I thought about what my dad had said to me while I was there at his house that day. I felt like I had done enough and that it was time for me to at least try to get myself together so that I could be the one to take my child to school on the first day. I had a friend by the name of Mr. James who was Shalamars father. Shalamar was only a year old, the other child that went to the foster home with Ivan. While I was with Mr. James, I was telling him about why I couldn't let him see his son, and about this addiction that I had and that I needed to go to the drug program. I told him that I needed to go right then. Mr. James Told me that he would take me, but he wanted some sex for the ride. Commenced, took me to a program located on Main Street, I stayed there for two weeks, Charles would see me after work some weekdays and on Saturdays. after the first two weeks of being in the program I got kicked out. The reason I got kicked out is because I was pregnant, and you couldn't be pregnant in this program. I called Charles he came and picked me up and asked me why I was putting my things in the car. I told him that I had to get kicked out because I was pregnant. Charles did not say a word to me all the way home and I did not say one to him either. I knew I had truly messed up on Charles, my marriage was not strong and by this time Charles was tired of me and fed up. We never discussed me being pregnant because Charles already knew it was not his child because he and I hadn't been intimate in almost a year. When I got put out of the program I did not run back to the streets, I figured I had a little head start and that I should keep on trying to stay clean. Two weeks wasn't much, but it was enough to make me put forth an effort to continue to try to get more clean time. I went to a program that would let me be there while I was pregnant, this was my fifth child, and I did not want to have a crack addicted baby again. I finished the program just before the baby was to be born and finally, I had my first clean baby. I was so happy I had accomplished something constructive. When the baby was born it was March 7th, 1995, my fifth and final child. I named her Imyunic James, she was perfectly normal, and she was the prettiest little thing that you ever did want to see. I was happy and I vowed that I would stay clean and sober, take care of my child, and raise her the way she was supposed to be raised, and do whatever I had to do to get the rest of my children. This time Mr. James wanted a paternity test, we did the paternity test 3 weeks later. when the results came, they came to my stepmom and dad's house. I got the mail and it read, "In the case of Imyunic James Howee James, it has been determined by this court, that Howee James is not the father." Oh my God. I acted just like a contestant on the Maury Povich show. I screamed, I cried, I was so hurt, and molded. I immediately called Mr. James and told him about the results. I was totally confused; I didn't think I had been with anyone else. I cried and cried and cried in the arms of Mr. James. He felt sorry for me because he asked me if I wanted him to act as her father. I told him yes because I needed somebody to help me with this child. I had already left Charles and was staying at my stepmom and dad's house with Isaiha and Asia. The following month I had made six months clean, and I was looking good, feeling good, had a little weight on me and had done everything I needed to do to get custody of these two children. So now I have custody of three of my children and I am still living at my dad's house. The feeling of motherhood was wonderful. Although I did not have any children by my husband, he still loved me. He hated the lifestyle that I was living, He had no idea that I had six months clean, I never discussed it with him, he genuinely loved me for the person that I was when I wasn't getting loaded, at least the person that I was before he knew that I was getting loaded because I was getting loaded the whole time until I told him myself. Shortly after having three kids for one year, the social worker asked me if I was ready to get my other two kids out of foster care. I had been going to visit them regularly, I was always on time, and I always had something to bring to them. I would take the other three children to visit with their two brothers. I was convinced that I could do it and in three weeks I got my two children Ivan and Shalamar out of foster care. The Department of Children and Family Services helped me to get a place for me and the children. Charles moved out of our apartment and went to Apple Valley, we were separated. Although I could have used his help, but I didn't think it was fair to him since none of the children were his biological children. I felt like since I did him so bad that I should just go ahead and live my life without him and just take care of my children. Living in our new home was great, we lived in Los Angeles off Manhattan Place near western. I got a call one day from the foster parent, the mother she asked me if we were OK and if I felt like I could manage it, you know having all the kids and doing what I'm supposed to do as the mother. I told her that we were doing fine, and again thanked her for taking care of my two boys. She went on to tell me that my sons were her 98th and 99th children. She told me that she wanted to get her one 100th child but she wanted to make sure that I was OK. I assured her that I was ok and that she could get her new foster care child. I thank God for that lady, because she didn't even have to call me to see if I was OK. The next time I called the foster parents somebody answered the phone and told me that they both had passed away from sickness. Some months down the line my aunt Lenore called me to see if we were OK. She asked me If Ivan and Shalamar could come to her house for a while, while I take care of the other children. I thought it was a good idea and I allowed her to come pick them up. Over the course of some time, I got a call from the hospital. The person on the phone told me that I needed to come there because my son Shalamar was there. When I got to the hospital my son was dead, I did not know what happened, but the hospital said they would do an autopsy…. When the autopsy report came back, it said that my son had cerebral malformation. In my mind I believed that someone had hit him in his head, or he hit his head on something hard. After this I got Ivan and took him with me. I couldn't be mad at my aunt Lenore because maybe it was just his time and maybe from the sounds of it maybe his cranium our brain was not fully developed. I was heartbroken it was the worst feeling a mother could ever have. my baby was gone, nothing could bring him back and all I could think of is if I had let my child stay home with me then maybe he would still be alive. I will never know. I had recalled the conversation that I had with the foster parents about them getting their 100th child. I wondered If the foster parents had passed away and told God that they wanted my child to be their hundredth child. I am sure it doesn't work like that but that's the thought that I had in my head for quite some time, and I was angry about it. Hurt beyond repair.

Chapter 6

Nervous Breakdown

10 days later we had Shalamar's funeral. Soon it would be time to check all the children in school. I was still hurting and mourning over my Shalamar, kids were at school, and I was lonely but surrounded by the thoughts of what really happened to my child. I didn't want to think about it. I wanted to be numb. With these starts running rapid for a whole month, I began

to have thoughts of relapse. It was then that I started to realize that I was motivated to get loaded behind things that triggered. The loss of my son really was becoming a thorn in my side, and before you know it, I was loaded. It happened suddenly one day when the kids came home from school, they were doing their homework and I was preparing dinner. The children watched a little TV and when they were all sleep, I had gone out the house, down the block a bit to where I had thought I saw drug dealers. This time I did not let my addiction get out of control. I did not use every single day like I did before I had the children. I would only use when those thoughts of my child would arise, I can't say that it was very often, but amount of time being on crack is not good, especially having young children. I felt like God was helping me. Of course, I would pray that my usage did not get out of hand like before. I went online and found a drug program. Although my drug use had not got out of hand, I still felt like I needed to go to an inpatient program. This program was only six months and my stepmom and dad agreed to keep the children. I have been in the program for two months, every day staying connected with the children. We were mandated that we had to call our children once a day. Everybody in the program had their own individual slot time to call their families. I enjoyed being in the program. The third month was my turn to work in the kitchen. I found out that I didn't know anything about cooking. It was my opportunity to gain experience on how to make different and delicious dishes that I could share with my children when I got home.

My dad had paid my rent at the apartment for 3 months. He started to feel like it did not make sense for him to have to pay rent at my house and at his own house. He took it upon himself to contact my property owner and tell them what I was going through. The management let me get out of the lease so that I could do what I needed to do to get better. I was grateful for that although when I got out, I didn't have a home to go to. The children were fine, they enjoyed being with their grandpa and Carol. It just so happens that one day in the program we were all in our class. The instructor of the class says today we are going to work on the thing that hurt you the most. I was a full-grown adult now. I realized that what grandpa was doing to me all those years was not supposed to happen. I'd always think about it and sometimes used it as a trigger to get loaded. So anyway, I had to think of the thing that happened to me that hurt me the most. I chose child molestation from my alcoholic grandfather. He had used me most of my childhood life to perform acts on me for his own sexual gratification. I was victimized and scarred for the rest of my life, so I decided to write about that. The instructions for this assignment were to write an essay about the thing that hurts us the most. There was a 25-question page that we had to answer each one by one in the form of an essay. 1.) what is your name?

2.) Where we're you born? 3.) what was the thing that hurt you the most? So on and so forth, as I answered the questions, I began to shake. By the time I got to the 10th or the 11th question of 25, I started to get a headache, was incredibly nervous and discontent, I could smell my grandfather's alcohol on his breath, and I could hear everything in my head that he had ever said or promised me. I began to cry and shake, I had passed out in front of everybody it was an embarrassing situation, but I didn't know about it because I was out. When I woke up, I was at Augustus Hawkins Mental Health Facility. When the program asked me for my emergency contact, I gave them my biological mother's information. Helen Ford and her phone number. The hospital wanted to know what happened from the treatment program. The hospital requested whatever had triggered this episode. It was the paper that I was writing, the exercise that was supposed to help me get over my hurt. Just because people are licensed in these facilities don't mean that they know everything, to me it was the worst thing that anybody could have made up to do about someone's pain. I'm pretty sure that it worked for someone and that's a great thing. When the hospital got the paperwork on what I was working on at the drug treatment center, they had to share it with my mother so that she could understand what I was doing when the incident took place. Mom did not come alone; mom did not drive so she asked her sister to take her to the hospital. When I woke up the next morning my auntie Evelyn and my mom was sitting there on the side of my bed. I was happy to see them, mainly because I had not seen them in a long time. After I got up and got myself together, use the bathroom, washed my face, and brushed my teeth, it was time for me to tell my side of the story. I began to cry; my auntie Evelyn asked me why I was crying. I told her that I was embarrassed because my grandfather had touched me on more than one occasion when I was a little girl and I let it go on without telling anyone. It was then that I found out that it wasn't just me. The first thing Aunt Evelyn mentioned was the fact that my grandfather had done the same thing to my mother while they were listening on the other side of the door. I had already known about this Prior to this incident. Auntie Evelyn told me that her father had been like that for a long time before I was even born and that it wasn't my fault. She told me that I was innocent. Auntie Evelyn told me a story about how her friends used to come over to do homework with them, and one day when her friend got ready to go home, my grandfather said that he was going to take her home. The little girl got in the car with him, and they took off. Usually after school grandma would let them go outside and play for a while, well they were in the yard and they looked down to the corner and they saw their friend an hour later after my grandpa was supposed to had taken her home, they saw her getting out of the car. Auntie Evelyn said the next day when she got to school, lots of children were looking at her strange because the young lady that grandpa was supposed to be taking home touched her, she told everybody that my auntie Evelyn's father was a dirty old man, and he was nasty. Auntie Evelyn told me from that day till the time she graduated from high school that she had to walk around the school with her head down and she could not be around her friends anymore in fact they were no longer her friends all she had was my mom, her sister. Oh my God, she had stories after stories about my nasty ol grandpa. Mind you, my mother never uttered a word, she was very soft-spoken and never talked about anything that happened. Auntie Evelyn also told me that my grandfather would make his wife do sexual acts with women so he could enjoy the view. It reminded me of how he acted the first time I had sex with K, my lesbian lover when I was in high school. I should have gotten in trouble for having sex in grandpa's house. Instead of him disciplining me and putting K out, he just stood there and looked, he was touching himself too. Nasty grandpa, perverted. Auntie also told me that grandpa had lost his mind for real. He was driving his truck one day and his mind snapped and left, he hit a brick wall and never came back to himself. Grandpa had Alzheimer's disease or dementia he got so bad till he thought that his socks were snakes, he'd scream and holler like he thought he was going to get eaten alive. Eventually grandpa had to go to the convalescent home. Grandma would always ask me if I wanted to go see him with them. The next time she asked me I went, finally I had a chance to forgive him. I fed him his lunch, rubbed him on his bald head and told him I forgive him. Three days later, grandpa had died. While I was still in the mental health, I had plenty of time to think. I was still in mental health for a couple of days. Auntie Evelyn and my mom's coming to visit me was the best thing That ever happened to me. I felt truly blessed to know that I wasn't the only one in the family that had been preyed upon. So it was time for me to leave the facility. I never went back to the drug program because of the embarrassment of what had happened. My dad and Carol still had my children, I was considered homeless because dad had given up my apartment and I wound up renting a house on 71st and Main St. I thought the children were going to come live with me right away, but they did not. My dad had them in some afterschool activities and they stayed at his house until the summer.

Chapter 7

Lynda

I had been separated from Charles for quite some time. I had no intentions on calling him, or trying to get back with him, or continuing as his wife. I was having flashbacks on my relationship with K. Of course, K was long gone and out of the picture I didn't even know where she was and didn't care. When I left to go to the military is when our relationship ended. I never spoke to her again even up until this day. I wanted to meet a woman. Someone that I could be close with and have a relationship with. I got on a chat line called date hook-up and met a young lady; her name was Lynda. Lynda was a married woman. When I started talking to her, she told me that she was tired of her husband, and she wanted to meet a nice woman. Well, here I was. Of course, by this time I had done a lot of drugs and some of the things that I did and said we're not sound. Meaning I was still a hot mess. During our phone conversation Lynda decided that it was time for us to meet. We hit it off well, and she often talked about leaving her husband to be with me. One day she came over and spent the night with me. The next morning when it was time for her to go home, I did not let her go home with her bra, in fact I didn't even let her take a shower, she smelled like hot sex. That way when she got home and her husband saw that she did not have her bra he would probably get mad and assume that she had cheated and would quit her, that's exactly what happened. She had nowhere to go… Duh.

that was the plan, I have accomplished just what I had acquired to do. I asked her to be my woman and that was that. She cooked and cleaned the house every day. She was content with watching her soap operas and listening to good music. She was a sex machine and she had to have it. Dad had the kids, and I had this new relationship, and this woman had to have all this great sex, and what is it that goes good with sex? DRUGS! One day my stepmom called me and said the baby wanted to come home. Imyunic wanted her mommy. I explained to Lynda that my daughter wanted to come home and be with me she understood and her and my child got along very well. We were in the year of 1999, Imyunic was 4 years old. Her nickname was Mookie. Mookie had never been around me while I was loaded. I have now been a drug addict on and off for almost 10 years, I started using in 1990 right after leaving the military. Mookie was always up under Lynda. That gave me plenty of time to run in and out the bathroom getting high, and she never even knew the difference, I am speaking of Mookie. Eventuality

Lynda Started to tell me that I wasn't spending enough time with her, and she wasn't getting enough attention. She would threaten to cheat on me. I didn't care I just wanted to be high. I didn't really believe that she would cheat anyway. I should have believed it because she cheated with me on her own husband. I have met a young lady name Dee, I have beat my girlfriend to the punch, I had cheated on her with Dee. I had only cheated one time with this woman. The next time I left with Dee it was on the last day in December 1999. Tonight, I am going to party like it is 1999, that's what Prince said. That day I had gone out to lunch with Dee, when I got home Lynda was gone. This was the absolute first time she had ever left and gone anywhere without me. Sometime ago my cousin Hogan had been living with us he fell on tough times, and we allowed him to come. Hogan used crack cocaine as well! That day when I got home, and my girlfriend wasn't there I called her." hey what's up love, where are you?" she said she was at her sister's house, because she wanted to spend time with her before the new year came in. I did not see anything wrong with that, she told me she'd be home later that night, and it was all good. By the time it got to be 9 PM

Lynda called me and said that she was waiting for a taxi, and it was taking long because it was New Year's Eve. She said her and her family were celebrating and having an enjoyable time. Oh, me I was smoking crack. Mind you nobody knew if the world was going to end on the last day in December in 1999 so everybody was getting their party on. 11:00 PM came and my girlfriend was still not home. I got done using and went to bed. It was January 1st, 2000, I picked up my phone and I dialed *69. "Hello" said the person that answered the phone. I said, "what's up may I speak to Lynda?" The lady on the phone said," why are you calling for Lynda" I said" is this her sister?" She said," No, this is Lona, and she ain't here, and she ain't been over here."" do not call my house no more. "I said," hey lady I know she's over there because I dialed *69 and this was the last number that she called from," put her on the damn phone". "She hung up in my face. All hell was about to break loose. I got myself dressed, got a screwdriver, put it in the waist of my pants and got on the bus. I was on my way to this woman's house. I knocked on the door, and said," Open up this door before I blow the hinges off of it." The lady said," no don't shoot up in here, my babies are here, and Lynda just left she called herself a cab!!!" I was so mad, even though I pretended my screwdriver was a gun. I got back on the bus, headed home and my girlfriend was in the bathtub. My cousin Hogan and Imyunic were still sleeping. I went in the bathroom, snatched her out of the tub, and asked her where the hell she was, she lied, and said she was at her sister's house. I have thought about the fact that I plugged up the curling iron just before I walked out the door." where was you, you better not lie, where were you?"" I told you Lisa, I was at my sister's house, stop I'm trying to take my bath. B stop lying," I ran in the other room and got the curling iron and I put it to her face, and I said, "I am going to ask you one more time," Where the F where are you?" I absolutely could not believe it my top was blown, I burned her with the curling iron on her arm. The sound of her skin sizzling was enough to scare the both of us. I had really burned her, she screamed for dear life, I made her shut up, she was standing there butt naked, I put her on the couch and spit luggies in her face, threw nails at her, then I called Lona while she was sitting there. Lynda never knew that I went to her friend's house. At least not until I started talking to her. I said, "Hey Lona; Lynda is swearing out that she was at her sister's house will you please tell me what happen with you and Lynda last night?" She told me everything while she sat there and listened. She even stated that she had sex with her with a cucumber." Ugh," I exclaimed, I told Lona thank you and got off the phone. I had gotten mad all over again," I thought you love me." "I do love you Lisa

I do." I told her you don't love me you love who you spent the night with last night." call her back right now and tell her you love her." "No, no, no, I love you" "NAW", you love who you spent the night with." "Now call her and tell her you love her!!" She picked up the phone, called her, and said," Lona, Lisa told me to tell you" — I had cut her off saying" don't tell her I said it you just tell her that you love her because you do." Lynda said," I love you, Lona!" I went off to Brazil, I had told this woman to call this woman and tell her that she loved her, and then turned around and beat her up for saying it. I slapped her so hard till she Peed on herself. I hung up the phone and said since you love her you can have her. Let's see if she wants you after today. I did not hit her anymore, I handcuffed her to the front door butt naked, and went to bed. Before I laid down, I said to Cousin Hogan "I need to go to jail for what I just did to that woman. I left her there handcuffed butt naked to the door and her son came to visit her and found her there. Someone called the police, I should not have done it because I knew that it took a lot to unlock the handcuffs, and if I wasn't unlocking them with my key then the only key that could unlock them were the police keys. I woke up two police officers in my face with guns drawn. I was arrested and they took me to jail. when we got to the parking lot of the jail, I was unclear about what my charges were. They had left me in a car next to another car that had two guys in it. The police officer asked what I was in for, and the police officer said, oh she is in for attempt murder. It was a heck of a shock to me. I thought to myself, "damn why am I in here for attempted murder I didn't try to kill anyone!" Well in Lynda's mind, it did seem like I was trying to kill her. Besides that, I did not know what she told the police, she may have lied. The police took me out of the car and put me in a cell for interrogation. When the interrogation officer came in, I told him the truth and nothing but the truth. I had told him everything that had happened, what I did and why. I could have gotten life in prison without the possibility of parole. They decided to drop my charge from attempt murder to corporate punishment on a spouse with great bodily injury. The public defender told me that it carried a maximum sentence of 17 years. I needed help. There was a lady named Bishop Sandra L. Hanna, she had a drug program called The Hanna House. The next day when I woke up and was still locked up at the jail, I called Bishop Hanna, and I told her that I really messed up this time. She asked me what happened, I told her that I had gone to jail for attempted murder, and they dropped it down to Corporal punishment on a spouse with great bodily injury. I told her I was looking at 17 years. Bishop Hanna said, "do you believe that the Lord can get you out?" I said no because I had really messed up this time. She asked me where was my faith? She assured me that she could get me out and asked me for the information for court. She came to the jail to visit me, and while she was there Lynda was also in the line. Bishop Hanna wound up getting into an argument with Lynda about the fact that she put me in there, and she was trying to go in and see me, while Bishop Hanna was trying to get me out. Bishop Hanna dismissed her from the line and came on into the jail and spoke with the attorney. on the day of court bishop Hanna came and told the attorney to let her speak to the judge. After she talked to the judge, the judge threw the case out and I left a free woman with Bishop Hanna. All the charges were dropped and for the next six months I stayed at the Hanna house. On the way to the Hanna House, we stopped off at the house on 71st St. I opened the door, everything in the house was gone, including my daughter and cousin Hogan. I went next door to the property owner to find out what had happened. The property owner told me that he realized that the house has been abandoned for quite some time, so he emptied out the house and got it ready for the next tenants. I apologized to him and explained that I had gone to jail. Luckily, I didn't get an eviction. Of course, Lynda left that house the same day I got arrested. It was told to me by one of my family members that she had gone to stay with her sister. I knew where her sister lived, in fact, it was right around the corner from Bishop Hanna's Hanna House. Day in and day out while I was still at the Hanna House I would always think about Lynda. I missed her so much. I remembered her cell phone number and one day out of the blue I called her. I was afraid that she was not going to talk to me. She told me that she was so glad that I had called. She asked me where I was at and could she see me. When I told her what street I was on she told me that she was right around the corner. I told her that I would let her know when she could come over. I never told her that I was at the drug program. The Living quarters for the Hanna House were merely an apartment complex. Lynda would not be able to tell that it was a treatment center. One day when Bishop Hanna left, I called her over and told her to go in the back of the house and come up the stairs. When she knocked on the door, I let her in. I told her that I did not have long for her to be there and we talked for a bit and had sex. Every day after that I talked to Lynda on the phone. She asked me if she could come over again. I told her no and told her what type of place it was and that I was not supposed to have her there in the first place. She then asked me if I could come over there to her sister's house, I told her that I was not allowed to leave. She did not care about that, she told me if I do not come within the next two days that she was going to call Bishop Hanna and tell her everything about her being up in the complex and us having sex. I overlooked it, and I did not talk to her again. This little hussy got the number to the Hanna House, called Bishop Hanna and told her everything about her being up in the complex, she told her exactly Where every picture was on the wall and what the picture was, how the bathroom looked, and what type of hand soap it was. I was busted, I was in trouble. But I did not get kicked out. Bishop Hanna: she was a real woman of God, and she forgave me for everything. True to this day, over 20 years later I am still good friends with Bishop Hanna, I stay connected with her. I am so grateful for her helping me out of every negative situation. Today she is called Chief Apostle Bishop Sandra L Hanna.

Chief Apostle Bishop Sandra L Hanna

All Praises to my Lord and Savior Jesus Christ, for placing this remarkable woman of God in my life. I am grateful for everything she has done for me, throughout my journey of addiction.

She is an overseer of many churches across the states. If it were not for Chief Apostle Bishop Sandra L Hanna, I would have gotten 17 years in prison. That means I only would have been out of jail for five years. Who knows I could have died in prison; the bottom line is I am blessed because of Chief Apostle Bishop Sandra L Hanna.

She was a real woman of God. Do not get me wrong, when I did this hideous act There were consequences. I had to write Psalm 119 10 times. Psalm 119 was the longest chapter In the Bible, it had 176 verses. My fingers hurt, And I was grateful, not angry at all. I learned a whole lot about that scripture, and I learned that you did not want to mess with Bishop Sandra L Hanna. When I finally left the Hanna House I went to my dad's house where my children were. when

I got there, I found that Lynda had taken a job from my niece, taking care of her twins during the day. My niece lived directly in the back of my dad's house in the back house. I never went back there because I still felt some type away about her telling Bishop that she had been up in the complex at the Hanna House. It was about a week that Lynda and I had not spoken, I'm not even sure that she knew I was there. I don't even know how she found out. The next day when I woke up Lynda was sitting in the chair in the same room where I was sleeping. When I got up and got cleaned up a bit, she asked me why I had not come in the back to see her. I told her that I didn't think she wanted to see me, after she got me in trouble where I was living. I will admit that I was still kind of angry and I didn't really want to have anything to do with her. Of course, I could have sex with her anytime I wanted to. Weeks went by and she started to get angry because I was ripping and running the streets and not paying any attention to her. I did not have an income because once you go to jail with Social Security, they stop your check. I needed

Lynda to make sure I had everything I needed while I did not have an income. She started to use the fact that I had no money against me, and she would tell me if you don't do this or that I'm not going to get the things that you need. One day she told me if I did not have sex with her that she wouldn't buy me tampons when my period came. I got so mad at her because she hurt my feelings with that, and I slapped her. I made a conscious decision to take my children and move to Apple Valley where my husband was living.

Chapter 8

Apple Valley

I had been talking to Charles and telling him about the things that I had gone through while we were separated. Charles and I did not get back together. But me and all the children went to live in his house until I could find another place to live. Charles had so many women running in and out of his house. I did not know who was who, or who his girlfriend was. Since

Charles told me it was okay for me and the children to come there all the shenanigans had to stop. He was dealing with a lot of Caucasian women, for me it was easy to get them to stop coming to his house once I announced that I was his wife. There was this one chick that really did not get it. She kept coming, and he kept letting her in. I see him give her money, and he even let her take showers anytime she wanted to. I did not like it and I told Charles that I was going go ahead and take my Children and find me a place. I looked in the paper under rentals and shared housing. There was a man that had a whole house, and he was looking to rent out two of the rooms. I went on down to Social Security and got my income started again. The first thing I did was buy me a car. The man that had the room for rent lived on a street called Saratoga, we stayed there for four weeks and then we found a place it was around the corner. It was a three-bedroom one bathroom house. When we got ready to move to the new house, we could not afford to rent a U-Haul and still pay first and last so since I had a car now, I decided to move everything by car. We didn't have that much stuff anyway. The only thing that was hard to move by using the car was the mattress for the bed. One of my sons's friends were over the day that we got ready to move. I decided that I was going to put the mattress on top of the car and go ahead and take it to the house, since the house that I found was right around the corner. The young man asked me if I wanted him to sit on the back of the car and hold the mattress down. I told him that would be fine, then here comes my daughter asking can she help. I told her NO! let the boys do it you are too little you're a little girl. She insisted that I let her help and I did. She sat on one side and held down the mattress and the young man held down the other side. As we were approaching the corner, I got ready to turn and when I was Halfway into my turn the mattress slipped off, and so did my daughter Asia. I had to take her to the hospital and there I was questioned about what happened. I told the truth. Took my baby home to the new house cared for her until she got better, and everything was OK. I thought until the police came to my house to get my statement about what had happened. I had already told the people at the hospital, and I wanted to give the same true story. After the police left my house, I did not think that anything was going to come out of it and that everything was okay now. Three days later I wanted to smoke. This would be the very first time that I had all the kids at the house smoking crack. I called my friend Denay,

Denay Johnson

(Clean, Sober, & Saved)

I used to live next-door to her, she was my hairdresser and my dope smoking running buddy. I called her and she came by to see the new place. She liked it the kids liked her, and they knew her already. We decided to get something to smoke, when we went and got it and came back, we went up in the room close the door and commence to doing what we did. We got so high till we got paranoid. Every time we would take a hit, we both would run to the window. It was a natural reaction for a tweaker.

The effect that crack had on us made us think that somebody was coming. Someone we knew and did not want to see or to see us loaded like we were. It could have even been the police. I was so tired of running to the window to peep out of the curtains. I told Denay next time we take our hits let's do something we haven't done before, this time when we get ready to do it, we're going to sit side-by-side and neither one of us is gonna run to the window. she said OK, and we tried it. We took our hit, looked at each other and hopped up and ran to the window.

That was enough for me for one night. I was tired all I wanted was a shower and to go to bed. Denay may have gone home or continue having her fun. Four days later Denay called me and asked me if I wanted to ride with her to the spot. I told her "Sure come get me I need one right about now." I have been so busy with the kids; it was Friday, and I was ready. When Denay came to get me, we went to the spot, got what we needed, and we were on our way back to my place. The kids were doing their own thing and paid us no mind, when we had finished that round of smoking, we left again to get more, on the way back the police pulled Denay over for a broken taillight. She had the dope in her bra and transferred it from her bra to a cup of water that she had been drinking from. When she pulled over for the police, they took the car and impounded it with the crack still in the cup. Denay went to jail, and I had to get home the best way I knew. I walked home, and I did not get high anymore that night. You might ask why Denay went to jail in the first place. The reason she went to jail is because when the police attempted to pull her over and turned on the siren for her to pull over, she didn't pull over right away, she panicked because she had the dope on her and was simply scared. We knew that not pulling over right away was admittance to guilt." pull over Denay "She said "I can't pull over what am I gonna do with the dope", I said "I don't know but we can't be in a high-speed chase." Well guess what, we were and that's why she went to jail we were originally getting pulled over because she had a broken taillight. when Denay got out of jail six days later for refusing to pull over she contacted me and asked me if I had gotten the cup with the drugs in it. I told her that I didn't get it. Denay came to the house and someone else's car and asked me if I wanted to ride with her to get the cup out of the car from the impound. I thought she was going to get the car, but she told the attendant that she wanted to just get some things out of the car and get the car later. She grabbed a sweater a couple of other things that she needed and grab the cup with the dope in it. It was like resuming where she had left off the night of the arrest. This wasn't the first time we had gotten pulled over by the police. The next time we had went to cop, in other words went to buy some crack we were driving in Denays car, and I was the driver with no driver's license. We got pulled over because I ran the stop sign. Hell, I was high. Denay did not know that my license was suspended, asked me what they did with the dope this time? She swallowed it. When I called her from the jail with my one and only phone call, she told me that she swallowed it." oh no Denay! "She asked me how she could get it out, I told her to drink a whole gallon of water and make herself throw up. And that is just what she did, and she was high all night. I got out of jail one week later. I had to do five days for driving with a suspended license. For me that was enough. I did not want to go to jail anymore. I stayed sober for three weeks and had a lot of time with my children. One day I had a knock on the door it was two cars of police, and I was under arrest for child endangerment and causing great bodily harm to my child. My child, Asia, hit her head on the concrete and had bleeding on her brain! OMG!!! Jesus Help me. this was a serious offense especially since I was a mom. When I went to jail, I spent my time at twin towers until my court date. I never mentioned my little brother Andre, he was nine years younger than me and had flipped his car five times and crushed his skull. He passed away and the day of his funeral I was on my way to prison. I wonder why I couldn't do a year at twin towers, instead of going to prison. I came to find out that the charge was too serious for county jail. I had to do prison time. I was truly scared to go to prison but that's where I had to go.

Chapter 9

Fugitive

I had a serious felony, and I was in the jail with the kidnappers the rapist and the killers. I had gotten a year, and I hoped that it would go by fast. I was so afraid that I went to the nurse and told the nurse that I had mental health issues and that I couldn't be on the yard with everybody else. I told the nurse that I was on Zoloft and Risperdal she made it possible and mandatory that I take this medication three times a day, at the same time every day. I snored bad, and my stomach gave me hell about it every day. I manage to do my year and when I got out the prison sent me to parole at a halfway house in San Bernadino. I was required to go to 12 step meetings every single day. The people at the halfway house did not provide a ride they said we had to get there by any means necessary. I knew that I wasn't going to be able to make it, so I hopped the fence and went to my dad's house in Los Angeles and I stayed in Los

Angeles running from the police for 10 months. Mind you when I got to Los Angeles, Lynda was still in the back house taking care of my niece's twins. I went in the back to see Lynda; we were cool as just friends. When I wasn't with her, I was in the front with the kids or, getting loaded. ripping and running all over again up and down the streets of Figueroa. Mind you, I was a fugitive I was supposed to be living in San Bernardino at the halfway house and here I was in Los Angeles with full-blown addiction going on. When a parolee is running from the police, they lose their Social Security. Once you turn yourself in and do your time you can get your money back. I wasn't ready I ran the streets for 10 whole months. The cold thing about being around Lynda and her knowing that I was on parole she tells me she was going to call my parole officer on me whenever I didn't do something she wanted me to do. She's also would say if you don't do what I tell you to do you're going to be one bloody Woman because I'm not going to buy you any tampons or pads. That was so dirty, and it really pissed me off.

Every day she would do something to make me madder. One day she said something foul, I pushed her, and slapped her, and guess what? She slapped me back; it was the first time she has ever hit me. we got into a little scuffle, and it was done for me. I went in the house, and I told my stepmom that I am tired of everything. I'm tired of running from the police. I'm tired of dealing with Lynda, I'm tired of not being a good parent for these children of mine, and I'm going to kill myself or kill Lynda. Carol Hopkins, my dad's wife, had just saved my life. Carol told me do not go in the back anymore. Go ahead and turn yourself in and when it's all over and you get out don't deal with Lynda anymore, leave that crack alone, and do what you got to do for these kids. At this point I was so ready to get all of this behind me. I called Charles and told him that I was coming out there and I wanted him to keep the car until I got out of prison. I told him that I was going to turn myself in because I was on the run. I thought that I could find a program that would take me, I thought I would be able to go to the program and call the parole officer and tell him that I was in a program. But when I called this particular program, they were asking me if I was on parole, and I said yes. The person asked me was I running from parole, I told her yes, she asked me where I was staying, and I told her my husband's address. I truly believed that I was going to Apple Valley to get in the program, I think the lady from the program told my parole officer that I was at Charles house. It was two hours later, and the parole officers were coming into the yard. We were sitting outside, and I just stood up and put my hands behind my back.

When I got to the prison, the next two days were court. This type of court was for people that had violations. There was a line of us, maybe 12 of us, inmates going in and coming out saying they got five years, two years, 16 years and more, when it was my turn, The Lord must have been with me. To tell you the truth he was with me all the time. The judge gave me 90 days, three months. In three months, you only have to do 1 month and 19 days. I was so happy I didn't know what to do, I felt like that was giving me a second chance, and I wasn't going to let Him down this time. I was determined to do what needed to be done. When my sentence was over, I did reside in Apple Valley. My dad brought the kids to me, and I knew that I couldn't do anything to mess up this opportunity to be a good mother. I enjoyed spending my time with my children. I never looked back; Lynda was the furthest thing from my mind. I had decided that I needed to go to church and take the kids with me.

Chapter 10

Frankie

One beautiful summer day, in the year of 2003 after my children and I got all settled into our place in Apple Valley, I needed to get groceries, enroll the kids in school, and start searching for a church that we could go to and get involved in. I was so grateful that I had another opportunity to do life the way it was supposed to be done. I felt like I was delivered from crack cocaine and now I was determined to live a righteous life for Jesus Christ. What I needed was a good church to go to. I had no clue. As I walked around the grocery store, I saw a woman with oxygen, she was trying to get a watermelon. She looked to be struggling, so I offered to get it for her. As I handed her the watermelon, I asked her if she was affiliated with any of the churches in the area. Come to find out she was, and she was also the minister of music. That was right up my alley because I love to sing. Singing and having an opportunity to be around other believers was right up my alley. I was sure that church would help with my drug addiction and provide a positive avenue. Learning new songs, and possibly leading a song one day was what I look forward to. The lady's name was Frankie. Frankie gave me her phone number and the address to the church. The following Sunday the children and I made it to the church early enough for Sunday school. The kids went to one class, and I went to the adult class. At the end of Sunday school, I met with the children Sunday school teacher, her name was sister Manthis. When sister Manthis brought the kids to me she said" dang you're kids are bad." I was offended, but not really because these children have never been in church. I said, "well, ain't this the church"" can't y'all change that" it didn't matter at the time because we all were looking for a change. That Sunday I heard the pastor say" Faith comes by hearing and hearing by the word of God." I had no clue to what that meant. all I know is it sound good to me. It sounded positive, and it sounded like there was hope for me because I was in despair. that Sunday after we got home from church, I had a received a call from Frankie." Hi Lisa, how did you enjoy the service?" I said" oh hi, hello the service was very nice, and we are coming again next Sunday." Frankie was delighted and she told me that there was also Bible study on Tuesday and asked me if I wanted to come. I didn't go to Bible study that Tuesday, but the following Sunday I did join the church shortly after that I went to new members class and when I completed it, I joined the choir. That all sounded good to me and that's exactly what I did. The kids seem to like going to church and they were learning a lot from going to Sunday school. Each Sunday I had learned a little bit more and was happy that I was staying clean and sober. The next person that I met was scooter. she was a very nice lady, and I could already tell that she would be in my life for a lifetime, today I called her my big sister. Scooter knew that I didn't have very much to wear to church, she asked me is she got some things together for me to wear and would I accept them. I was happy, and told her that I would, and she told me when she got them all together, she would call me. That Thursday would be my first choir rehearsal, I learned three new songs, I learned that wherever we were at 12 noon on Saturday that we were supposed to have a unity prayer while everybody in the choir was in their separate homes. We were supposed to bow down in prayer to God for the services on Sunday. I like the idea; Frankie told us that We were praying on Saturday at 12 noon for the unity of the choir and for us to be on one accord. She taught us that we were not performing. It was called rendering songs of praise unto the Lord. The following Friday after Sunday services, Frankie called me and asked me if I would like to do lunch. We went to a nice restaurant not far away. I didn't think anything of it. It was very peaceful, and I felt safe and was happy that Frankie invited me. While we were eating Frankie asked me how long I had been in Apple Valley. I told her that I was only there one week before I met her at the grocery store. She asked me why I left Los Angeles. I told her that I needed to start my life all over again, fresh and new. I told her that I had been on crack for a long time and that I was in a lesbian relationship with a woman who I was very abusive to. I also told her that I had been in and out of jails and I just wanted a new life. I expressed that I was tired of living a sinful life and I wanted to give God a chance to change my thinking and my heart. I wanted to be a better mother and learn how to be a real Christian and hang out with other believers. I felt like I shouldn't have told her everything, but I did. I think the reason why I told her everything because I was releasing it from myself. I was kind of embarrassed because everybody doesn't take kindly to lesbianism, and I had hoped that Frankie wouldn't start treating me differently. I felt no change in her treatment toward me as the days went on. Until I got the next call from her a week later, she asked me if I wanted to go out to dinner after rehearsal the following week. I told her, "Sure" and we went out that Thursday evening after choir rehearsal. Frankie busted my whole entire bubble. Over dinner she told me that she was lesbian, and she wanted to lay down with me.

My heart was beating so fast. I couldn't believe it. I knew that it was a tactic and a trick of the devil. I knew that Satan would do anything to take my focus off the opportunity that I had to live a righteous life with Jesus Christ. Frankie, the one person I thought I could confide in, who I thought my secrets were safe with. Flip the script and wanted me to lay with her. I had a bittersweet feeling, I couldn't eat anymore, and I was curious. I had fell for the okey-doke. From that day I stopped focusing on trying to get better and live life according to God's will. I was back in my own will again. I don't know why I had allowed this to happen, but it did. every day I would talk to Frankie on the phone. Whenever she wanted to come and get me, I would go with her she treated me nice, at first. Then it started to seem like she was Lynda all over again. The very first time I went to her house I was very impressed, she had a big house, with really nice things. The house was two-story, she had three children, two boys and a girl. And her bedroom she had a waterbed, and I couldn't wait to get in it. I hadn't been with anyone since I turned myself in from running on parole. I felt excitement all through my body. I have lost all focus on what I was supposed to be doing. Spiritually, I still went to church and sang in the choir. The first sexual encounter I had with Frankie was awesome. She was very experienced and very smooth about the way she handled me. I had never had sex in a waterbed, but it was nice. That's what I look forward to the most Frankie 's waterbed. Frankie was not out as a lesbian to her children, or to the church. In fact, she told me that if it ever came out that we were having an affair that she would definitely deny it. Of course, I never thought that it would get out and I sure didn't want it too. As we lay after the first encounter her son knocks on the bedroom door, I am naked, and she tells me to get in the closet. I did it and I couldn't believe I was a grown woman hiding from a kid in the closet. I stayed in the closet until Frankie finished talking to her son. I believe I stayed in there for 20 minutes. I need it to be at home with my own kids. It was time for me to go, and she took me home, we talked late night about our incident, she loved it and so did I. we continue to meet up for more than a years' time. Frankie started to change on me. I came to find out that Frankie was abusive in her own little devilish ways. The first sign of devilment was when we were supposed to pray at 12 noon on Saturday. I was at her house this Saturday and we were sitting at the table. I said Frankie it's 12 noon it's time to pray. Frankie said I know it's 12 noon, but I want you to come here! I couldn't believe it, but I went to her. She kissed me and led me to her bed and all of a sudden, she did what she does, this time it hurt me really bad. I asked her" why are you doing that so hard it hurts." Frankie told me that she wanted it to hurt so that when I walk, I would think of her. it was weird and I was angry about it, she got angry because I wouldn't answer her calls after that happened. One night I called her and apologized for not answering her calls and told her I missed her, and she came to pick me up. When she came to pick me up I had to get out of the car and walk down the side of the house and climb up a pole to the balcony. I wonder if it was that serious for me to be with her that I would have to climb up a pole to get to the balcony. I guess that proves that I would do anything to be with her. I stayed with her all that night and just before daylight I had her take me home before my kids got up for school. Soon as both of our children were at school, she called me, and she wanted to talk. Our conversation turned into an argument, I found out that Frankie could really act out when she's mad. It was a sad thing because I had nobody I could tell or share my feelings with about her. Of course, I had Scooter, CC and

Carlisa. We were all in the same choir together. Scooter and Carlisa adopted me as a little sister and CC was like my role model. These ladies are still very important in my life. They were all very nice Christian women, and I did tell CC and Carlisa about what Frankie and I had been doing, and some of the things that she had done to me. Carlisa listened to everything I had told her. The next day she called CC, she listened attentively but she never said a word. Everything that Carlisa had said to CC was the exact same thing that she had already heard from me. Carlisa decided that something needed to be done, she called the pastor and made him aware of the fact that Frankie the minister of music is mixed up in some sort of lesbian relationship with another member of the church. I don't know what was said, but I knew that the pastor would call me." hello" ""Hey listen, I need to ask you something" "What is it Pastor?"" is it true that you and Frankie have something going on? "I was honest and told him yes. Pastor thought I was lying because Frankie had denied it. Frankie told me that if it ever came out, she was going to deny it. and that's exactly what she did. The pastor, I thought would have taken both me and Frankie into the office and had a conversation with us about it. Unfortunately, it didn't happen that way. The pastor called a meeting with the choir. Frankie was a good musician and I'm sure Pastor did not want to lose her, she played the keyboard and directed the choir, picked songs for the leaders and she could really sing well. I did not. I don't know why the Pastor did not take us both to the office, most likely that bothered me for so long.

If we had gone into the office the three of us, I am sure the truth would have come out. By Pastor bringing members of the choir to this meeting allowed the people that didn't know anything about the affair and to have the opportunity to know all about it. How embarrassing it was that way. I believe that if the Pastor would've taken us both in the office then he could've given us some spiritual counseling, and guidance. I was told by several people what went on in that meeting, the pastor asked his questions, all of which I knew not. I do know that one question was how many people in here knew what was going on. I do not know, nor did I care. The strangest thing happened during the meeting. I was told that Dorothy McNair was recording by cassette player. All of a sudden in the middle of the meeting while Pastor was talking it comes to an end and clicks. Pastor heard it and asked what that noise? Dorothy McNair said that it was her and the pastor took the cassette from her. I'm sure after this meeting the people left saying wow!!, forward and wow!! backwards. Frankie and I were not speaking because she had treated me bad for the last time. I was angry with her because we had an argument and she put me out of her car, and I ran off and she did not know where I went. I got word that she was sick. In fact, it was breast cancer. before Frankie had surgery to remove the cancer. CC and another lady and myself went to visit Frankie. This was the first time I saw her after I jumped out of her car. Of course, I still cared for her, especially now that I knew she was sick. When we got to her house, sat down and we were all talking. Everything was cool until Frankie asked me if I was still mad. I told her a little bit yes, I am. She said "So what are you going to do, run off like you did the other day? "I instantly got angry all over again. I walked out of her house at about 9 o'clock at night. It was very cold. I had to walk 3 miles in a very cold frostbitten weather. I went to the crack house, got some crack and had the dope man take me home. Little did I know that CC would get in her car and set out to find me. CC went up one street and down the other. No Lisa, nowhere to be found. I was at home smoking.

Getting loaded and my vicious cycle of drug usage had begun all over again. I realize that things that got on my nerves, or that made me angry was a trigger for me. When I got home the kids were sleeping. CC knew I had relapsed because I had to answer her about my whereabouts. I did not lie about it.

Chapter 11

Crack At Church

Pastor did not know that I had a drug addiction problem, but he would soon find out. I continue to use, take care of my kids, and just try to go to church and continue doing what I was doing. Although I was a drug addict I still went to church and got the word and tried to learn it well enough to eventually one day follow it, and remember those clothes that

Scooter gave me, I wound up selling them when I ran out of money, she knew, because she never saw me wearing them. I just thank God she forgave me, by this time, I was getting crack on credit. I always paid my debt on the first day of the month. One day I was getting a ride home from choir rehearsal. I got a ride from Dorothy McNair; I asked her if she could take me to this person's house that had loaned me some money to feed the kids previously. I told her that it would only take a second. She didn't mind, but yet her light was shining right on the person's house. This was actually the crack house. I needed to pay my debt and buy some more crack. When I went in and told the dope man what I wanted. He told me to go tell the driver of the car to turn the lights off his house. I went out and asked sister McNair if she could turn the lights off of the house. She said, "no it's dark out here, we are in Apple Valley I'm not turning my lights out." I told her to just go on ahead and I'll walk home. I am only two blocks away I'll be fine. She asked me was I sure and I said yes. So, she left, I got my drugs and went home. The next week, Thursday, choir rehearsal I told myself I'm going to go and get my crack before I go to rehearsal. Then, I'd already have it. Whoever was going to bring me home wouldn't have to stop anywhere, and I'll be ready to smoke as soon as I got home. well, I came to realize that wasn't a good idea. I am at choir rehearsal sitting in the choir stand, and I got this crack in my pocket, and my pastor is in the building, he's walking in and out and utterly getting on my nerves. Why? Because I had the crack in the church and I felt like I had betrayed him. I knew it was disrespectful to him and God. The thought of getting loaded overwhelmed me. I was getting the heebie-jeebies, twisting in my seat and anticipating going home. Rehearsal was the furthest thing from my mind, although physically I was there. Pastor pops up again. He's sitting and looking at us rehearsed. My brain kept telling me he knows; he knows, go tell him you're quitting the choir. I attempted to go and tell the pastor that I was quitting. I left the choir stand and was standing in front of the pastor. I said, "Pastor, I need to get out of this choir." he said, "why?"," because I really have a back crack addiction, and I have a crack in my pocket." he said," do you really have crack in your pocket?" I said," "Yes I do" he said," well give it here" I said," The devil is a lie" "No…. I think that was the first time I ever said the devil is a lie." Pastor I'm just going to leave, I'll come back to the choir when I stop smoking crack." pastor said the unthinkable. He said, "Lisa listen here, don't you get out of this choir, you go home and do what you gotta do, but don't get out of the choir, because that's gonna be another hour you're going to be high and eventually you will start coming to church. "" You need this choirs support." I agreed and thought it was a great most marvelous idea. It was like a dream come true. I just gotten permission to sing in the choir, and smoke crack all at the same time and be high as I want it to be. My addiction got so bad to the point that I was getting loaded on Saturday night until very early in the morning. Most times I would take my last hit just before time for me to leave for church, sometime not even getting a shower. It was so bad that I wound up getting out of the choir, barely making it in the church doors on Sundays. I probably took my last hit at 6 AM on Sunday morning giving me enough time to come down a little before leaving for church. Many times, when I get there, I'd sit in the back by the ushers. Every Sunday I fell asleep and woke up by the time service was over. I'd even raise my hand and say hallelujah at the appropriate times. This is what I did for a year after the pastor confirmed that I could. Eventually the words of the pastor started to touch my heart and I had learned to listen attentively almost like I was in school somewhere taking a college course. The Bible really started to come alive in my heart, and I learned how to believe in Jesus Christ. I was learning how to let the words of the Bible change my heart, my thinking and the way I did things. I was changing from all my evil and negative ways to a nice young lady that was eager to live for Jesus Christ. I was able to do what was right, and when I fall into various temptations, I knew how to pray for God to give me a way of escape. I was filled with the Holy

Spirit years ago, that happened in the 1980s. Thankfully God kept me all those years. God often reminded me of how He kept me over the years of all my addiction and bad moves in the streets. I had become a good mother although I'd always left my children at home to fend for themselves, The Lord took care of them for me. He never let any of them get sick. God helped me to care for my babies the best way I knew how. Some years later the church had a picnic. I attended and my pastor called me over to him and told me that I looked very studious, and he knew I had learned a great deal about the word of God. It was at that moment that he asked me to become a Sunday school teacher. I was honored and humbled, I was ecstatic of the fact that he even felt like he wanted me to be a teacher. Learning how to present in class was very successful and I enjoyed it. By the time I had made a conscious decision to never touch crack again. I had gotten compensated from the United States Navy, it came through 100% disability due to post traumatic stress disorder. My children Isaiha, Asia, Ivan, and Imyunic we're all grown up. living on their own and doing life the way that life was supposed to be done. All my children did better than I did in their young adult years, I was very grateful for that. My youngest Imyunic was 20 years old.

Chapter 12

Family

In 2015 I got a call from my cousin Juanita. Juanita is my first cousin. My biological mom Helen was living with Juanita's mother in Pasadena. Her mother's name was Evelyn. Cousin Juanita called me and told me that her mom had gotten sick. She had developed cervical cancer. Cousin Juanita told me that I had to get my mother because Evelyn was going to be selling her house, and she would be taking Aunt Evelyn to her house in Moreno Valley to care for her. Auntie Evelyn had been diagnosed with stage four cervical cancer; Cousin Juanita took good care of her mom up until she went home to be with the Lord. It was still 2015, it was nice living with my mom and knowing that I would have her for the duration. Cousin Juanita told me to go and get power of attorney so that I could handle everything that needed to be handled, if anything ever came up. Everything was good. Eventually we moved to a four-bedroom home with a den. Imyunic, my youngest daughter came to live with us as well. I am recalling when Imyunic was in the 12th grade, she was failing in every class. I did not know what to do. I had a conversation with a couple that had helped me out with my son Ivan previously when he was doing bad in school. The couple were very nice to us. They'd always run to my rescue when it came to my children. They allowed my daughter Imyunic to live in their home for her 12th grade year.

Samuel & Unia Harris

Forever Grateful, Thank You!!!

They worked with her, and worked with her, and worked with her. She graduated with a good grade point average which landed her in Alabama State University. She stayed with us for a year and then got her own place. Imyunic became a medical assistant. Imyunic got a good job at the Adelanto prison and stayed there until she's switched jobs sometime later. Imyunic One day asked me who her biological father was. I told her really and truly I didn't know. I told her that we did a paternity test Howee James, and it was proven that he was not the father, so we left it alone. Imyunic did ancestry.com on her own, she met one of her cousins, and the cousin told her that it could only be one of two people. The first person was too young to be her father. The second one had to be him. Imyunic acquired a picture from somewhere and came to me and asked me if I knew the dude that was on the picture. You'll never guess who it was, it was the guy that lived two doors down from my dad. His last name ironically was brown. So, since Howee James last name was James, I just started calling her

James Brown. Asia had become an RN registered nurse after completing all her college courses and taking the state board test. Asia has a daughter who is named after her, her name is My "Asia Mosby, she got her first debit card when she was only 12 years old. My son Ivan Edwards married Tianna Spencer.

They are in their 10th year of marriage. I can recall speaking to Tianna years ago and she told me that she knew that she was meant to be famous, and rich, she was very serious about it and determined to make it happen. Tianna and Ivan are into the poly lifestyle. They became Facebook famous, they we're known on many social media platforms. They were known to have 1 or 2 girlfriends. Tianna first taught Ivan how to get paid on social media. Then she branched out to teach people all over the world, how to become monetized on social media. Tianna is an influencer, that gives people advice on how to build up their social media, with viewers. She teaches her influencers that they have to have social media etiquette so that they could be successful in whatever social media activities they may have. Tianna's social media name is May Bae. Ivan's social media name is The Edwards empire. They have used other names as well, but these are the two most popular. This dynamic duo, they are very extraordinary, exciting and they live a very happy life for all the world to see. Isaiha is just Isaiha, he does whatever he wants to do when he wants to do it. Isaiha has 2 little girls, Aaliyah and Savannah Walker. I love all my children, And I am so grateful that they were able to rise above the way that I was raising them while crack addicted, and everything that came with it. I am grateful for each and every one of them, for never disrespecting me, or making me feel less than because of the way that they were brought up. Thanks be to God for His love and kindness and his tender mercy.

I thank you, my children, for their love and concern for me.

Life with my mother has been really rewarding. First and most importantly my mom has lived long enough to see me get clean and sober. My mom turned 80 years old on October 7th, 2022, my mom is very healthy, and she does good with only one eye to use. Sometime ago mom had a detached retina, and when they did the surgery to repair it, she lost her eyesight in that eye. Mom can't hear very well, and she wears two hearing aids. I take my mother to church with me every Sunday. She is not a member there. She is a member of a church in

Los Angeles to which she still pays her tithes. She has been paying tithes to this church since 1980. My grandmother used to play the organ in this same church as a matter of fact my family were the first members of the church in 1956. The church was called youth Memorial Church of God in Christ. The pastor of the church now always calls and thanks my mother for her tithes. I am grateful for him for recognizing her. We are now living life on Gods time. We get along very well and have never said a mean word to one another, we are very happy with our relationship, and we wouldn't have it any

other way.

Helen Ford

(Mommy I Love You)

My mother always says that I am the boss. In all actuality my mom is really the boss. Sometime later after my mom came to live with me, we were in the car, and I told her that I was going to stop over on Bear valley to see if my friend Michele was still over there. I had met Michele at the Library many years ago. I had given her my phone number and we talked from time to time, and she also went to church with me three or four times before losing contact. It was about 10 years later when Mom and I went to Michele's last known address. Michele was still there I was shocked, and I was happy to see her. I asked her what was going on and she went on to tell me that she was going to have surgery on her hip the next day and she needed a ride to her mother's house, so that her mother could take her to the hospital for her surgery. When Michele got to her recovery mode, she called me and asked me if I knew anybody that had an extra room. I told her that I did, and she's been living with us for just about five years. Michele and I get along so well, she looks up to me, like a role model. Michele and Mom get along good they are buddies. I am grateful for my life and everybody that is in it.

Chapter 13

Hope For A Future

I pray for people that are struggling with any and all issues that I had gone through as mentioned in the book. I don't want anyone to be held back from their full potential at being whatever God calls them to be. Finally, being a productive member of society feels good. I have no desire to turn back or ever use drugs again. I thank God for salvation, deliverance, and a relationship with Jesus Christ. For Jesus Christ came to seek and to save that which was lost. Jesus is the Way, the Truth and the Life, and those that seek Him, shall find Him I pray. "OK, what will be your next move? Who will you tell about the wonders of Jesus Christ Lord and Savior? Will you let Jesus lead guide and direct your path? May you and countless others find Jesus and let Him be the Almighty Master and Personal Savior over your life. May you all love one another as Christ has love us.

Chapter 14

Charles Walker

As you all may very well know, Charles Walker was my husband, and he is now in heaven with his Lord and Savior Jesus Christ. Charles loved me so much. He put up with a lot that he did not have to put up with. I was so selfish, and I always did what I wanted to do. Of course, it does not make it right. It was not my fault I blame it on drug usage. Charles did not deserve the disrespect that I gave him. He was innocent. I had no regard for his feelings and no compassion. I wish I had an opportunity to make it right. Unfortunately, he is no longer with us and all I can do is share this little poem with you that I wish he could hear.

I'm sorry Charles

I am so sorry from the bottom of my heart, my actions, the things I did were not very smart. I wish you were here I would tell you face-to-face, how God came and saved me with His love and amazing grace. You chose me to be your wife, and to my surprise. Held my face and looked into my eyes. Your love for me was really true, I was strung out on crack and didn't know what to do. Up one street and down the other, when I should have been at home being a mother. Five kids to be exact, but I was drugged out and addicted to crack. So many nights I left the home, you looked around and I was gone. Oh, my Lord please come rescue me, resist the devil and he will flee. Charles, I am so sorry for breaking your heart so many times. While in the streets smoking dope and committing crimes. In and out of jail, and prison too, locked up for a year, what was I to do. Charles I'm so sorry, it didn't have to be that way, if I only had listened when you said baby let's pray. If I had a chance to fix things, that would be great, but now you are with Jesus, and it is all too late. Someday I will see you again, when I reach heaven's gates.

Chapter 15

Scriptures Of Apology

Confess your faults one to another, and pray for one another, that he may be healed. They effectual fervent prayer of a righteous man availeth much.

Matthew 5:7 Blessed are the merciful, for they shall obtain mercy. A new covenant I give unto you, that you love one another, just as I have love you, you also are to love one another.

2.) 2nd Chronicles 7:14 if my people who are called by my name humble themselves, and pray and seek my face, and turn from their wicked ways, then will I hear from heaven and I will forgive their sins and heal their land.

3.) Isaiah 55:17 let the wicked forsake his way, and unrighteous man his thoughts, let him return to the Lord, and he may have compassion on him, and to our God for he will abundantly pardon.

Isaiha Walker

Asia Hopkins

Ivan Edwards

Imyunic James

Shalamar James (Deceased)

(When Im Gone, "Yall All Yall Got")

To my children and countless others, I thank God for every one of you, for being in my life and helping me along the way. I have not always been the mom that you all know today. Many of you know me before my addiction, during my addiction, and after my addiction. You have all played a very important role in my life. I'd like to apologize to all of you whom I've have hurt, lied too, miss treated, stole from, and who I may have said all manner of evil too. I am sorry from the bottom of my heart. I know many of you did not deserve to be a part of some of the things that

I have done. If you're reading this and you can remember that one thing, please know that I've asked God to forgive me, and now I am asking you to forgive me as well. I am glad that the change in my life came before I left this earth. I am grateful that I did not die in the streets due to my drug usage. I'd like to apologize to all of my children especially for being irresponsible and careless in your upbringing. I was wrong, I was selfish, and made a lot of mistakes, been in jails, in prison, drug programs and more. Literally I left my babies to fend for themselves.

I ask you to forgive me for using mind altering substances that rendered me incapable to function on a mature adult level to care for all of you properly. Neglect, abuse, abandonment, and times when I ignored and discarded your feelings. Times when I could not help to properly bring you up and raise you the way I should have. Not showing love and affection when it was needed. I apologize sincerely with everything in my being. I pray that the positive changes that I have made in my life, can help me make up for the time that we have lost. We cannot get these very important personal childhood years back, if there is anything that happened to you that shouldn't have while in the care of others, I do apologize for being absent at the time. Today in my life you all very well know that there is nothing that I wouldn't do for you, in my possible power. We can cherish what time we have together, I praise God for you all, and to God be the glory for the things that He has done. Thank you again for loving me the way that you do, each and every one of you are special to me. Let's go forward and be loyal and loving, striving to be the best that we can be. Putting God first, relying upon His Word, and having a relationship with Jesus Christ our Lord and Savior. Love you very much.

Thank you

Chapter 16

Substance Abuse

There are many drugs in this world. Drug addiction is very popular in our world today. Drug abuse is the same as substance abuse. Drug abuse, and drug addiction starts in the brain. The brain has a neurotransmitter which sends messages to the brain. One of the neurotransmitters, which is called dopamine. Dopamine is the portion of the brain that makes people feel good and want to do a thing repeatedly. Thereby causing a drug addicted person to have drugs as their main interest. Impulsive behaviors and emotional responses get stronger and stronger and makes the ability to make decisions weaker. The body develops physical dependency and without the use of drugs the drug addicted person will experience withdrawals. Drug addiction in teenagers or in young adults happens because of pressure in school and stress in the home, neglect, abuse, divorce, death of a loved one, money trouble and addiction that is already present in the home. Drug addiction also causes depression and social anxiety. Many young people develop habits of drug addiction because of poor coping skills, curiosity and sometimes mainly to just have a good time. Peer pressure also plays a part in drug dependency and drug abuse. Repeated use of drugs can cause changes in the brain, make life worse and increased addiction can cause people to go to jails and even death. Drug addiction causes the addicted person to be dysfunctional. One out of ten adults suffer from drug addiction today. people that use drugs by shooting it in their veins with a needle risk catching HIV, hepatitis B and C. Signs of a crack addiction are physical and physiological changes, weight loss, discolored teeth from usage, irritation, lack of sleep and some people that suffer from drugs abuse try to hide it because of the embarrassment of drug usage. Drug addiction is not good because it causes families and relationships, to break up. When parents of young children become drug addicted it causes the children to be rebellious and out of control. drug addiction is a very serious disease, it requires treatment of the mind body and spirit. Addiction is considered a drug disease, because it affects the way the brain works. People who are drug addicted experience loss of control, they lie, and they are deceitful. Many have relapsed after trying to quit. When a person is trying to recover from drug addiction, they need treatment with health education and family support. The national Institute on drug abuse (NIDA) is the largest supporter on research of substance abuse and addiction. If you know someone who is in danger or drug addicted and need/want help, please seek immediate attention by calling 911 or poison control 1-800-222-1222 for treatment, 1 800 662 – HELP for www.findtreatment`.gov.

I have seen many people die as a result of drug addiction or drug abuse. I am grateful to be here to write this book and share my story with you. at this time, I'd like to share some scriptures that have to do with drug addiction and how we can turn to Jesus if we ever run into this problem. Spiritually the Lord can help you or your loved ones who may be in distress due to drug addiction.

- 1st. Timothy 5:8-provide anyone who does not provide for their relatives, and especially for their own household, has denied the faith and is worse than an unbeliever.

- Psalm 33:1 Unity, behold how pleasant it is for brother into dwell together in unity

- Psalm 127:3-5 behold, children are a heritage from the Lord, the fruit of the womb is a reward. Like arrows in the hand of a warrior, so are the children of one's youth.

4. Hebrews 11:1 now faith is the substance of things hoped for, and the evidence of things not seen.

5. Romans 12:2 do not be conformed to the pattern of this world but be transformed by the renewing of your mind.

6. 2nd Corinthians 10:4 for the weapons of our warfare is not carnal, but mighty through God to the pulling down of strongholds

7. Jeremiah 17:14 tell me oh Lord and I will be healed, save me and I will be saved, for you are the one I praise.

. Proverbs 25:28 a man without self-control is like a city broken and left without walls

. Titus 2:11-12 For the grace of God has appeared bringing salvation for all people, training us to renounce ungodliness and worldly passions, and to live self-controlled, upright and Godly lives in the present age.

Ephesians 6:1-17 Finally my brother, be strong in the Lord and in the Power of His Might. Put on the whole armor of God that you may be able to stand against the wiles of the devil. For we wrestle not against flesh and blood but against principalities, against powers against the rulers of darkness of the world against spiritual wickedness in high places where for take onto you the whole armor of God that you may be able to withstand in the evil day, and having done all to stand, stand therefore, having your loins girded about with truth and having the breastplate of righteousness and your feet shod with the preparation of the gospel of peace, above all taking the shield of faith, Wherewith you shall be able to quench all the fiery darts of the wicked. And take the helmet of salvation and the sword of the spirit which is the word of God praying always with all prayer and supplication in the spirit and watching there unto without perseverance and supplication for all the saints.

Addiction, cravings, drugs, alcohol and acts of the flesh are only temporary. Only in God will you find eternal life. Only in God will you find strength to overcome and move on to a happy healthy life. There will always be Temptations along the way, but only God matters through Jesus Christ our Lord and Savior.

Chapter 17

Thank You Lord

To My Lord and Savior Jesus Christ…….. Jesus my Lord and Savior! I give Praise and honor and glory to you, thank you Lord for delivering me from all my troubles and misfortunate situations. Thank You, Lord, for your love, kindness, grace, and mercy. Your unmerited favor and protection. Thank you for renewing and restoring my mind body and soul. I praise your name Lord Jesus for the opportunity to write and share my life with others. Thank you for keeping me alive and allowing me to overcome so many challenges. Lord I still have issues and I'm trusting you to be the Lord of my life. Thank you for your Son, Jesus Christ who died on the cross for my sins, and countless others thank you for raising up early Sunday morning with all power in your hands. I thank you for your shed blood, for without the shedding of blood there would be no remission of sins. To God be the glory for all these things.

Lord Jesus, please watch over everyone that struggles with some type of drug abuse. Please bless them to realize that you love them so much, and you're willing to save them from their sins. Lord touch their hearts and cover them with your blood. Hold them in your loving arms, touch them from the top of their head to the soles of their feet. Lord be a mind regulator and a heart fixer for those who are struggling with all types of addictions. Lord in the name of Jesus restore relationships, mend broken families, and broken hearts. Those children who are victims of the effects that drugs have on their parents and loved ones, Please Lord in the name of Jesus protect them, they are innocent. Let some souls come crying" Lord what must I do to be saved. "Lord please protect the mental health patients, homeless and those behind prison walls. Lord in the name of Jesus make Your Word come alive for people of all nationalities, all over the world. Save them Lord in Jesus name I pray Amen!!

It's nice to have good friends, Those who will be by your side when things get tough, Those who will hold you accountable for your mess, that will pull you up when your down, That give words of encouragement, and don't say all manner of evil against you falsely, who show ginuine kindness, concern, love and respect, My very best friend who has been there from the time I moved to the Apple Valley area has something she would like to say.

Journey

I am ecstatic with the achievement of Ms. Lisa Hopkins in the completion of her book. I have known her and have been in her life for many years. I've witnessed several serious ups and downs during the course of our friendship. Many may ask my reasons for never giving up on her, it was because of her resilient faith. I'm grateful that I could see beyond turmoil that would cross her precious life. The tears and laughter were real, and I cared enough, and loved enough to be by her side. Her determination to pick herself up, denounced those things that weren't truly who she really is, this caused me to embrace her with love and honor. She loves hard, and I am blessed to call her a true friend, one that I could call upon and depend on. Lisa, baby girl, I am so proud of you.

The door is open, now walk boldly through it.

God bless you dear heart, and congratulations

on a job well done.

always and forever.

your very best BFF!

LOVE,

Min. Carolyn A, Coley

P.S It's A Process

Chapter 18

Poem: Jesus Conquers All

Jesus conquers all, He does it every day. With his love, and kindness in such a special way. Born of a virgin just to die. He had to do it to save you and I. 1 cross 3 nails, in hands, and in His feet, dropped his head, gave up the ghost and the mission were complete.

Three days you stayed in the grave. When we were lost to seek and to save. A Crown of Thorns was placed on His head He has risen He is not dead.

Jesus conquers all. And that's what he'll always do. Making intercession to the father for me and for you. I thank God for His sacrifice. His only Begotten Son Jesus the Christ.

Quality of living, quantity of time. Give your life to Jesus, or it won't be worth a dime.

Study the word, to show yourself approved, be humble, be steadfast and be unmoved.

Don't be moved by those bringing stress, stay on your guard and always do your best.

Jesus conquers all, He was the only one that could. Read your Bible and pray and do what you know is good. No time to play the worlds shallow game, to miss the Rapture would be such a shame.

Jesus Christ, He's my superstar, hold your head up, walk in your purpose and know who you are. This life is so short so do the right thing, so you'll be ready to meet with the King of Kings.

Jesus conquered all on the cross the day He died, let Him in your life today He'll always be by your side. Holy, Holy Hosanna to the Risen

King, clap your hands, pat your feet, open your mouth go head and sing.

Read the Bible, let it minister to you, for its light, not dark, it'll tell you what to do.

This book of the law shall not depart, read the words, and hide them in your heart.

Mothers and Fathers teach your kids to pray, a relationship with Jesus Christ in these last and evil days.

Jesus is Almighty, He will never let you fall. When you call His name, He will answer when you call. Jesus Christ is Lord and Savior, and He conquers all.

As I once heard before, which that I find it all true, in this world I'm living.

1 Cross 3 Nails = 4 given

Declaration

I Lisa Hopkins, declare that the stories in this book are true. These stories are not meant to hurt anyone's character or reputation. This book has been written to share my truths and life experiences. This book is not meant to offend anyone. The purpose of this book is to present an avenue of escape for those who may have encountered or may in the future encounter the shortcomings mentioned in this book. Many of the names have been changed to protect me and the person who is characterized in this book. May God get the Glory for all souls saved because of this book.

Concordance
Scripture Reference Page

1. Addiction   Ephesians 5:15
2. Addiction   Proverbs 25:28
3. Addiction   Romans 13:17
4. Apology   1 Peter 4:8
5. Apology   Psalm 34:14
6. Apology   James 5:16
7. Child molestation Ecclesiastes 4:1
8. Child molest station Matthew 18:6
9. Children   3 John 1:4
10. Children   Isaiah 49:15–16
11. Children   Matthew 19:14
12. Children   Psalm 127:3–5
13. Church   Ephesians 2:19–20
14. Choir   Colossians 3:16
15. Comparison   1 Peter 3:15
16. Crucified with Christ Gal. 2:20
17. Devil and Sin 1 John 3:8
18. Discouragement to children Col 3:21
19. Deceit   1 Peter 2:1

20. Deceit Ephesians 5:6
21. Deceit Jeremiah 9:6
22. Drug addiction 1Corinthians 6:17
23. Drug Addiction 1 John 2:16
24. Drug Addiction Romans 12:2
25. Drug Addiction 1 John 2:16-17
26. Faith Romans10:17
27. Faith Hebrews 11:1
28. Forgive one Another Colossians 3:10
29. Give thanks in all things 1 Thess5:18
30. Gods Promises 1 Peter 3:9
31. Grace and Mercy Hebrews 4:16
32. Great day Jude 1: 24
33. Holy Ghost Acts 2:4
34. Jesus is Lord Philippians 2:10–11
35. Lesbianism Leviticus 20:13
36. lesbianism 1 Corinthians 6:9–11
37. Lesbianism Romans 1:26–27
38. Love 1 Corinthians 13
39. Love for Jesus 1 John 4:19
40. Love one another John 13:34
41. Marriage Hebrews 13:4
42. Marriage 1 Peter

43. Mental Health   2 Timothy 1:17
44. Mental health   Galatians 5:22–23
45. mind   Philippians 4:6–7
46. Marriage   1 Peter 4:8
47. Military   Isaiah 4:10
48. Military   Jeremiah 29:1
49. Military   John 14:27
50. No condemnation Romans 8:1
51. Partiality   Acts 10:34
52. Provision for family 1 Timothy 5:8
53. Relationship   Revelation 3:20
54. Resistance   James 4:7
55. Respect   Matthew 7:12
56. Respect and Hope   1 Peter 3:15
57. Renewing the Mind   Romans 12:2
58. Salvation   Acts 2:38
59. Selfishness   James 3:6
60. Selfishness   Proverbs 18:2
61. Selfishness   Mark 12:31
62. Sex   1 Corinthians 6:9
63. Sex   2 Corinthians 12:
64. Sex   Ephesians 5:3
65. Sex   Ephesians 5:6-7

66. Spirit of the Lord   Isaiah 59:19
67. Strength   Ephesians 6:10
68. Stronghold   1 Corinthians 10:4
69. Troubled Times   Psalm 17:17
70. The Beginning   Ezekiel 26:36
71. The devil   1 John 3:8
72. Theft   1 Corinthians 6:10
73. The Lord is   Psalm 23
74. The Lord's Prayer   Matthew 6:9–13
75. Train up a Child   Proverbs 22:16
76. Undefiled   Hebrews 13:4
77. Whole Armor   Ephesians 6:10–17
78. Wisdom   James 1:5
79. Unity of Family   Psalm 133:1
80. Zeal   Galatians 6.9

www.ingramcontent.com/pod-product-compliance
Lightning Source LLC
Chambersburg PA
CBHW060110170426
43198CB00010B/840